REVOLUTION IN THE CITY OF HEROES

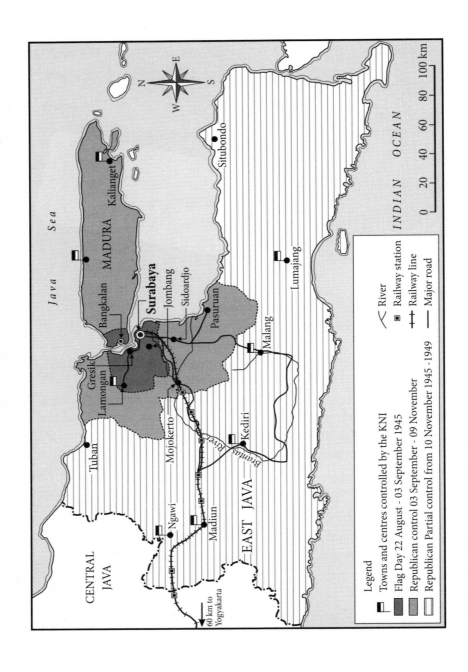

REVOLUTION IN THE CITY OF HEROES

A Memoir of the Battle that Sparked Indonesia's National Revolution

SUHARIO PADMODIWIRYO

translated by

FRANK PALMOS

RIDGE BOOKS
SINGAPORE

© 2016 Suhario Padmodiwiryo and Frank Palmos

Published under the Ridge Books imprint by:

NUS Press
National University of Singapore
AS3-01-02, 3 Arts Link, Singapore 117569
E-mail: nusbooks@nus.edu.sg
Website: http://nuspress.nus.edu.sg

ISBN: 978-9971-69-844-7 (Paper)

National Library Board, Singapore Cataloguing-in-Publication Data

Padmodiwiryo, Suhario, 1921- author.

Revolution in the city of heroes : a memoir of the battle that sparked Indonesia's national revolution / Suhario "Kecik" Padmodiwiryo, translated by Frank Palmos. – Singapore : NUS Press, National University of Singapore, [2016]

pages cm

ISBN : 978-9971-69-844-7 (paperback)

1. Padmodiwiryo, Suhario, 1921- 2. Revolutionaries – Indonesia – Biography. 3. Surabaya, Battle of, Surabaya, Indonesia, 1945. 4. Indonesia – History – Revolution, 1945-1949 – Personal narratives.   I. Palmos, Frank, translator . II. Title.

DS644.1.P24
959.803092 – dc23   OCN915326975

Cover design by Nelani Dd Jinadasa; Typeset by Pressbooks
Printed by: Markono Print Media Pte Ltd

CONTENTS

Preface   vii

Acknowledgements   xvii

1. Planning Our Revolution   1

2. Tearing of the Tricolour   27

3. Arms Raid at Don Bosco   49

4. The Fall of the Kempeitai   63

5. The People's Military Police Force   84

6. Three-Day War   108

7. Death of Brigadier Mallaby   138

8. The British Ultimatum   153

9. The Battle for Surabaya   172

Epilogue   199

Author's Note   203

Afterword   204

PREFACE

World War II seemed without end for Indonesians in 1945. In Europe and the United States there was dancing in the streets after Germany surrendered on 7 May 1945, but in the Pacific and Asia the Japanese fought on with suicidal desperation, costing tens of thousands of lives. Even after their formal defeat, Japanese occupation troops remained in Indonesia, armed and in control. The Japanese emperor's reluctant surrender broadcast of 15 August, after the atomic bombing of Hiroshima and Nagasaki, had failed to change the status quo.

The Japanese used ridding Asia of European colonial powers as a pretext to occupy Indonesia. The Dutch colonial government quickly fell, leading to a three-year Japanese occupation. After the 1945 surrender, the former colonial powers of Britain and Holland began reasserting themselves. A war of a very different nature broke out in Java.

The Japanese had promised release from servitude, but in three years of occupation imposed an Asian-style colonial rule, far worse for native Indonesians than any experience under the Dutch. The nationalist movement had gained momentum during the occupation, accelerated by the brutality of the Japanese that impressed upon Indonesians that only full independence from any foreign power would be acceptable.

The victorious British-Indian Army arrived in Batavia, now renamed Jakarta, in September 1945 to accept the Japanese surrender, repatriate more than 70,000 prisoners of war, and reinstate the pre-war Netherlands East Indies Colonial

Administration. While waiting for the Dutch Army to regroup, the British seconded the defeated Japanese troops to help them put down independence uprisings. The Netherlands East Indies government leaders, who had safely seen out the war in Australia, also began arriving in September, declaring to the British that all Indonesian people would welcome them back as "parents".

But this was easier declared than done. Native Indonesians now wanted nothing less than complete self-government. The tide of sentiment for independence had risen during the occupation and the formerly embryonic nationalist movement had grown to immense proportions. The anti-Japanese feeling reached an even higher peak when the British and Japanese collaborated to crush freedom movements in Bogor, Bandung, Cirebon and Semarang from late September through October. The British comfortably controlled Jakarta, using British, Japanese and the first of the returning Dutch Indies troops to police the streets. Dutch civilians were returning and claiming back their former properties and assuming their former colonial roles.

The British and the Dutch were contemptuous of the 17 August Proclamation of Independence made by nationalist leaders Sukarno and Dr Hatta. To the British the document was very much a dead letter. And given that foreign forces were once again in charge, for native Indonesians the Proclamation now appeared more a statement of aspirations than reality. Only in the port city of Surabaya was the Proclamation treated as a serious call to action. If Surabaya fell to the British they would bring in the Netherlands Indies Civil Administration (NICA) to complete the reoccupation of Java by the New Year of 1946.

Long after the Japanese surrender the war-time Japanese news blackouts continued, so very few outside Surabaya knew that this city alone was upholding the spirit of the 17 August Proclamation. Surabaya youth (they called themselves "Arek Suroboyo") gradually coalesced into action groups, launching mass attacks to seize Japanese weapons and materials and take over military compounds. They knew that without weapons they could not possibly hold out against the modern, well-trained British-Indian Army, due to arrive in late October 1945.

The Surabaya demonstrations of support for the Proclamation began on 22 August 1945, today known as the Day of 50,000 Flags, when thousands of kampung people poured into the streets holding aloft thousands of hand-sewn, small red and white national flags which they pasted on light poles and buildings along the boulevards or flew over the bamboo, adorned gateways to kampungs. The Japanese were unable to combat this mass outbreak, nor could they withstand the mass ambushes that followed. Mobs carrying clubs, knives or bamboo spears targeted armories, demanding weapons. Among these ambush crowds was young Hario Kecik, who later described the masses as acting like "an organic body." Once the street fighters chose a target, the kampung intelligence network went into top gear. Kampung boys with no previous connections joined the street ambushes against Japanese guard posts, armories, vehicle compounds and also, selected killing of individual Japanese soldiers known for a history of cruelty.

Kecik's insider narration reveals that the Arek were not particularly disciplined or well organized, but their underground Intelligence network in kampungs and high schools was impressive. Within hours a crowd of more than 50,000 could be raised to ambush a Japanese compound. Very soon, nervous Japanese troops, fearing being torn to pieces by mobs, took passive stances and allowed the Arek to seize their weapons. It was not always easy, as this story will reveal, and the cost in young lives was high, even before the beginning of the Battle for Surabaya.

As the day of the British warships arrival approached, the Arek's desperation and bravery intensified and they brought down the hated Kempeitai secret police, a drama well told by Kecik, who was one of the first to take control of their headquarters building.

By late October those ambush and attack skills were well honed. British Commander Brigadier Mallaby had naively deployed his British-Indian troops into the suburbs to take over the city — breaking a pledge to the Republican leaders not to move his troops from the port. They were easy targets for mass attacks by the kampung people. Using crude weapons and light arms, the people had within 48 hours almost wiped out the entire British garrison, killing 600, with the remainder back at the base threatened with total annihilation. Mallaby appealed to Jakarta for help.

Local heroes abound in the Surabaya story of 1945, but their history was not well recorded. Colonel Sungkono, who led the militia forces, left an unedited batch of notes and maps which Jakarta historian Dra Irna Soewito processed into a three-volume, impersonal semi-biography titled *The East Javanese People's Defense of Freedom*. Governor Surio, whose defiant speech of 9 November remains today perhaps the finest of Churchillian style broadcasts in the Republic's short history, left no detailed memoirs. City Administrator Sudirman left incomplete diary notes for historians, and several notable freedom fighters left accounts of their experience, or were, like Bung Tomo, the radio propagandist whose broadcasts set nationalist emotions aflame, the subject of biographies written by others.

By far the best reporting of the negotiations between British officers and Surabaya's nationalist leaders was by Ruslan Abdulgani, who rose to great heights in the new Republic in later years, with his *One Hundred Days in Surabaya That Shook Indonesia*. But no one dealt with everyday events as well as young Suhario Kecik, who takes readers along with him on the formation of major strike militia and the mass ambushes of the Battle of Surabaya. At 24 years of age, he was a Deputy Commander in a 500-strong unit headed by his best friend, 28-year-old Madurese, Hasanuddin Pasopati.

Known throughout his life with the family nickname 'Kecik', Suhario was the brightest literary star to emerge from Surabaya, yet he too would have been unlikely to have put pen to paper but for a curious incident. In the early Suharto presidency years of 1968–70 he was detained upon his return from a military training course in Communist USSR. That he had also finished a similar course in the United States before going to Moscow must have later given the excitable anti-Communist New Order officers sufficient reason to tone down his sentence to a period under house arrest, a compromise that suited everyone.

For historians, this misapplication of Suharto's zeal was a blessing in disguise. The home confinement released General Suhario from immediate duties, gave him continued salary and the peace needed to start his memoirs on Surabaya. He sent out batches of letters asking his former colleagues for collaborative details of their Surabaya days. His home office in Bekasi, just east of Jakarta, soon had the appearance of a publisher's library hit by a whirlwind as the paper files stacked up. Kecik painstakingly wrote far more than the Surabaya story, which occupied just four chapters and 260 pages of his finished work of 730 pages, a 300,000-word manuscript that Obor Indonesia editors and the admired journalist Mochtar Lubis lauded generously. Lubis introduced the book as one every young Indonesian should read to learn of the great sacrifices the youth of 1945 had made for Indonesian independence.

The title was both inviting and misleading. *Memoar Hario Kecik, Autobiografi seorang mahasiswa prajurit* (Memoir of Hario Kecik: An Autobiography of a Student Soldier) is a memoir and an autobiography, true. But the "student soldier" part refers only to Surabaya, the focus of this translation. The post-Surabaya chapters deal with his successful life as a military officer, a career path he found a natural extension of his Surabaya fighting days, which began before the Republic had created its national army, the Tentera Nasional Indonesia, or TNI.

Hario Kecik's intention was to take young Indonesian readers along with him through his pre-war home life, his medical studies under the Japanese, his shared nightmares with other medical students, ordered to daily pick up bodies of enslaved laborers who had starved to death, and hardships of life in general during the occupation. Kecik and his friends were among thousands of ambitious Indonesian youths plotting against the Japanese, planning freedom, but stymied by the iron fist of Japanese rule. When the surrender announcement seemed to offer their opportunity for self-rule they are suddenly plunged not into a post-war peace but a different, new war against a new foreign enemy: the British-Indian Army arriving to restore the Dutch East Indies colonial rule.

In August 1945 Kecik returned home to Surabaya, rating it the Republic's only city with a chance of winning independence. By mid-October the British were in control in a very subdued Jakarta where the Dutch pre-war leaders were arriving and demanding Sukarno be arrested and tried for collaborating with the Japanese.

Suhario's *Memoar* remains the outstanding historical diary of the first steps of the Indonesian Republic. For pure, unselfishly written diarizing, nothing in Indonesian literature compares. It has no peer in Indonesian literature as a step-by-step record of ground level activity in the fight for independence that began with Surabaya's brief local independence at a time when the future of the proclaimed Republic looked bleak indeed.

It becomes a history in that it contains details historians had looked for in vain among other sources. British and American authors wrote of Surabaya, but from afar, using British press releases. British soldiers later wrote personal accounts of their experience that confirmed the intensity and brutality of the fighting. But the bigger story of how the Surabayans were able to organize and withstand the powerful British-Indian Army was almost unknown. A hint of the accomplishment came in the brilliant title to 1995 vignettes of the Battle by Barlan Setiadijaya — who also went on to a successful military career — *The Moment when Boys Became Men*.

But by 1990, forty-five years after the Surabaya violence, Kecik alone was left with the energies and talent to set down for the new generation a detailed story of Surabaya and how the city won its title as the birthplace of the Republic.

— — —

How this enhanced translation of his work came about is also a curious story. Most all of the best known Surabaya veterans had passed away by 2010, so I was astonished to hear at that time that Kecik was very much alive and writing a new book. I took the next plane out from Perth in Western Australia, carrying a video camera, to meet him in the Obor Publishing boardroom in March 2010 for the first of our five video sessions and numerous face-to-face interviews.

We soon worked well together, meeting at his Bekasi home or in Obor. Initially I consulted him for my own research purposes, for a substantial history to be titled *Surabaya 1945: Sacred Territory* [forthcoming]. After a time, we agreed to also work together on a revised translation of the Surabaya portion of his memoir.

This translation modifies the original *Memoar* published by Obor in 1994 in several ways. It includes important revelatory passages from videotaped interviews done in Suhario's home, as well as lines from scores of emails from him. From my own research I had more information from the period to insert into Kecik's published tale to round out the story for contemporary readers. Suhario agreed to numerous small inclusions of this sort and made other small amendments as we progressed.

The two inserts provided here originated with Ruslan Abdulgani whose civilian role for the Republic and as the representative on the Contact Bureau as secretary and recorder were thankfully later put into print in his *One Hundred Days in Surabaya that Shook Indonesia*. Kecik's description of the tearing of the Dutch flag over the Hotel Oranje, the bloody incident regarded by many as the start of the Revolution, was well expressed. But he knew of but did not witness an event the next day that was missing from his original Obor account. Governor Surio had sent Ruslan Abdulgani, who spoke Dutch, to Room 33 of the Oranje where he confronted the conspirators, warning them there would be serious bloodshed if they tried raising the Dutch flag again. The implication was that these Dutch officers would be especially targeted in the Oranje. When in Surabaya in 2010, I checked these details and visited Room 33, noting its vulnerability to any attack. Kecik was happy to include the small segment to round out the story:

The following day, Thursday 20 September, Ruslan Abdulgani, on orders from the leaders of the independence movement in Surabaya, went to room 33 in the Oranje. Standing in the doorway and speaking in fluent Dutch, Ruslan told the conspirators their lives would be at risk if they dared anything as stupid as raising a Dutch flag in Surabaya, ever again.

The second insert was also a Ruslan account that Kecik had known. Kecik had been impressed with British senior officer Captain Shaw's personal courage and bearing when Shaw had come alone to deliver a document to his compound, in a day of high tension. Kecik took care to see that Captain Shaw was given every courtesy and safely escorted back to "enemy territory." Shortly after, a humorous exchange took place, which Ruslan later told me about, in a personal interview in Melbourne. Kecik wished to insert the few lines because it would reinforce the impression he had of Shaw as an upright man, in circumstances where other British were seen as uncharitable and untrustworthy.

When Captain Shaw and Ruslan Abdulgani had been appointed joint secretaries of the Contact Bureau they met the following day. Ruslan surprised Captain Shaw by appearing in uniform with a Captain's rank, not his usual civvies. Captain Shaw asked:

"Mr Ruslan, I see you are in uniform. How long have you been a soldier?"

"I joined yesterday."

"Just one day and you are already a Captain!"

"You are a Captain, so they said I should be also."

The big difference, as I assessed the pairings (said Kecik), was that Shaw and Abdulgani were civilized, educated and polite men who would in peace time have become friends, whereas both Mallaby and Mansergh were unnaturally stiff in their approaches to our Governor, resorting to haughty postures that revealed inexperience outside of military training. Abdulgani was not a military man. He had only worn the uniform on instructions from Governor Surio and removed it soon after.

Kecik was correct. Shaw and Abdulgani became good friends when Ruslan visited London in 1956 as Foreign Minister. Shaw told his fellow officers that he would have been a general in a week if Governor Surio had raised Ruslan to a higher rank every day he wore the uniform!

We also agreed to trim details and lists of the scores of small militia units whose importance has faded. Kecik excelled in recreating the atmosphere of the times, a good example being his description of Sukarno's brief visit to Bung Tomo's Rebel Radio station on the eve of the Battle, where Kecik had escort and guard duty for the president.

We also collaborated by email up to June 2014 on his recall of emotions the day the war had ended, allowing me to build upon his descriptions of the eerie hours when he and his young squads, he agreed, "seemed to be in a trance, hardly daring to believe they could now stand upright and cross a road without being targeted by snipers."

If I have, as translator, missed relaying the full emphasis of a message that Kecik repeatedly made to me, it was to ensure the present generation of readers understands that the Surabayan people won this great defensive victory for the infant Republic. Kecik's book corrects the common, mistaken assumption that Indonesia was free from the day independence was proclaimed on 17 August 1945.

There was no formal military force in Surabaya, nor were there any religious or other dominant factions; traditional divisions along social lines were blurred. From Governor to kampung dweller, Republican forces were intent upon winning freedom, and were prepared to die trying. The people had understood Governor Surio's 9 November evening radio broadcast warning that in refusing to surrender to the British forces a great number of Surabayan people listening to the broadcast would not be alive to see the sunset of 10 November 1945.

No period of Indonesian history will better repay study than Surabaya in 1945, which saw the Japanese military occupation of the Netherlands East Indies come to an end and the foundations of a new era of Indonesian self-government begin.

This is the diary of a talented young man whose knowledge of both Dutch colonial life and Japanese military rule prepared him better than most for his shared leadership roles in the newly emerging nation. Suhario Kecik 's name will endure, generation after generation, as Indonesian society matures and scholars see the value in the preservation of such valuable documentation.

Suhario Padmodiwiryo was 93 years of age in May 2014, yet he remained in contact with me, providing helpful additional material and comments on his magnificent, original publication, as this English version was being prepared.

On his deathbed in Jakarta in 2014, Kecik told his loyal wife Dewi that he would now die in peace, knowing that NUS Press and Obor would publish his book in English for a wider audience. He died on 19 August.

ACKNOWLEDGEMENTS

Many colleagues permitted me to use information from their diaries and reproduce excerpts of their valuable experiences. For me that was not light work. When I was collecting material for this *Memoar* many of them were already dead. Those who died included Suyono Prawiro Bismo, Pramuji, Kusnadi, Susanto, Jakfar, Ibu Supiah, Muhammad Padang, Kusno Wibowo, Margono, Suyono Ongko, Selamat, Suryono, Harsono, Hartadi and Kusen.

The war against the British was by all people of Surabaya, aided by volunteers who came from all over East Java and the islands of Madura and Bali, combining to make this a truly heroic story. It was about freedom, not about an individual or even one group of people. Fortune had me playing central roles in these important weeks, but at other times I was a mere bystander, a hardworking deputy Commander seeking to be with my men and my superiors in the right place at the right time to help our nation toward independence.

—General Suhario Padmodiwiryo, July 2014

University of Western Australia Associate Professor Dr David Bourchier handed me my first copy of Suhario's original 1995 edition of *Memoar* in 2010. Knowing my long-held interest in Surabaya through my association with Dr Ruslan Abdulgani, one of the Republic's Founding Fathers, neither David nor Dr Stephen Dobbs, Chair of UWA Asian Studies, were surprised that I was on the next flight out to Jakarta after learning Kecik was still alive and writing, at 89 years of age.

At Obor, publisher Madame Kartini and editor Andreas Haryono, set up many videotape interviews for me with the uniformed General and his wife Madame Dewi, thus starting a long friendship. Kartini and Andreas also opened a disused rooftop garret on their building where I spent three days and nights writing the first first drafts of this remarkable work.

My 1960s student days friendship with Ruslan's daughter Retnowati led to my access to her father's unfinished work on Surabayan history, where the family played host to me for several weeks in 2010 and 2011. So many others who helped me with this historic work have since passed on, notably Rosihan Anwar, an eyewitness to the Battle for Surabaya and a friend since our first meeting in 1962 and through my later years as a Jakarta correspondent. When the going was tough, Alison Puchy's editing and positive appraisals of this difficult translation kept me on course.

—Frank Palmos, August 2015

PLANNING OUR REVOLUTION

SETTING THE SCENE: THE JAPANESE OCCUPATION

The Japanese Occupation of the Netherlands Indies (1941–45) began with a welcome from many Indonesians keen to rid themselves of the Dutch colonial administration. The Japanese Imperial Army had overpowered the Dutch, who had held the territory for two centuries. By 1943, however, the Japanese had revealed their contempt for the Indonesian people under their control, enslaving hundreds of thousands of villagers, confiscating agricultural produce and sending unpaid laborers to the Japanese Army in Thailand and Burma. They controlled all media, executed anyone caught listening to war news, and dismantled scores of steel bridges to send to Japan to be melted down for the war needs. Thousands of innocent people were summarily executed for minor infringements and beatings, including of women, were common. By the end of 1943 the people were wishing the Japanese had never come, seeing them as far worse than the Dutch colonial rulers. Both foreign rules had given rise to a strong nationalist movement led by Sukarno and Dr Hatta, who fought for self-rule as the better future path for the Indonesian people.

The Japanese landed in Surabaya on the First of March 1942, raising their flag over the Wonokromo Bridge. They began immediately to 'Nipponize' Surabaya, removing signs in Dutch or English, destroying Western films and books, and demanding Indonesians learn the Japanese national anthem and bow towards Japan to honor the Japanese Emperor. Suhario 'Kecik' was a medical student and early victim of the Japanese anti-Western hysteria that closed educational institutions in cities and brought misery to the entire population. In August 1945 the Surabayans turned on the Japanese, armed themselves, and prepared for a fight to determine their independence against the British-Indian Army attempting to reinstate the Dutch. Kecik was in the middle of the fray, first as a student planning underground moves, then as Deputy Commander of a 500-strong youth force that took on the British in the crucial Battle for Surabaya, 10–24 November 1945.

THE LONG JOURNEY BEGINS

The Anatomy Department...was by 1943 flooded with bodies of the homeless and those unfortunates who later became known as romusha, men recruited on rosy promises to help 'Brother Japan' in their war. They were in fact slave labourers used by the army. So many had died of ... exhaustion, hunger and beatings that the bodies soon piled high ... we had to stop taking delivery.

The Japanese Imperial Army marched into Surabaya on Friday 6 March 1942, announcing what would be a torrid, repressive three-year occupation by flying the Japanese flag over the Wonokromo Bridge. They closed the Medical School I had been enrolled in and other institutes of Western learning, so my parents suggested I go to the Veterinary School in Bogor, West Java, to continue my studies. They had also closed the Jakarta medical school; I had nowhere to turn, and Veterinary Science seemed the closest I could get to my desired profession.

I said goodbye to Hartadi, my childhood friend, without realising he would later play a major role in the Battle of Surabaya alongside me four years later. He had been offered a job in the Railway Workshop in Surabaya, so would 'guard' Surabaya for us while I went to Bogor, and of course we promised to keep in touch, neither of us guessing that his railway connections would soon become vital to the anti-Japanese independence fighters' network.

When I arrived at Bogor I discovered I was not the only Surabayan student there. Basuki and Bahar Razak, old friends from the Faculty of Medicine in Surabaya, were also there, so I stayed in a group in unfamiliar surroundings.

There was still a little pocket money secretly available to me from Hartadi who had what he called the 'Robin Hood funds' from a Dutch government office the Japanese had seized in the first days of Occupation. The senior Dutch and other office workers had fled as the Japanese soldiers blustered in, leaving behind a full cash box used for fees and taxes and the like. None of those fleeing wanted the cash box, so Hartadi, not wishing the Japanese to get it, carried it away, renaming it the 'Robin Hood funds' for him and his close friends. Used quietly, the funds lasted for many months and helped our circle of friends get through some nasty scrapes. When the Japanese were entrenched they printed their own paper money, which was soon useless and fell apart. Dutch money was illegal, but still the best guard against inflation.

The Robin Hood fund was not entirely used for altruistic ends. After especially enervating days, several of us would splurge on a memorable meal down at the main market. Alas, those meals became memorable for the wrong reason. It would be many years before we could again live in safety, or have adequate food or clothing.

We were in the Bogor Veterinary School for just a few months. The Japanese soon realised they would need to reopen at least one Faculty of Medicine because the Imperial Army would need a lot of trained medical and paramedical staff. Along with the Faculty of Medicine in Jalan Salemba which reopened in Jakarta in April 1943 as Ika Daigaku, (a name which nobody used), they also opened a Faculty of Pharmacy.

In Surabaya, where they had closed my medical school, they chose instead to open a Faculty of Dentistry, a decision which would come to haunt them in mid-1945 because Dr Moestopo, the chief lecturer, turned it into a school for amateur spies, whose intelligence gathering while posing as menials and waiters to the enemy was very effective. It became a "public secret" that we were eavesdropping on both Japanese, and later, Dutch conversations.

In the first months, our student dormitory or *asrama* was in a Christian middle high school opposite what is today Jakarta's biggest public hospital, the RSCM Cipto Mangunkusumo. The dorm wasn't big enough to hold all the students, most of whom were from outside Jakarta, so we crowded together while the new rooms were built.

The lecturers wore Japanese military uniforms, and, although we didn't then know all the ranks, we knew that one young surgeon, who spoke German, was a major. Major General Dr Itangaki, head of the Faculty, seemed sympathetic to Indonesian students, in contrast to most unsmiling Japanese. Suwadi, an older student who lived on the edge of town in Jatinegara with his wife and two children, seemed to organise everything, employing a middle-aged woman who prepared three meals a day for us. The food wasn't too bad, and the Japanese left the asrama management to Suwadi, which allowed us to concentrate on studies. Were we wrong about the Japanese? We had little cause for concern.

THE MOOD TURNS NASTY: HEAD SHAVING BEGINS

One afternoon after lunch, about 20 of us were lying on our bunks when one of our more conservative, polite and soft-spoken students came into the asrama loudly cursing the Japs. His head had been shaved, and he looked so odd we could not help laughing at him. "Shut up! What you don't know yet is that the Japs are shaving our heads! I tried to resist, but they did it by force. This is an insult to our race!" He spoke the truth. It was not long before we were all shaved and as unattractive as the Japanese soldiers.

The Japanese had wanted us senior students to form a 'leadership group' and drill publicly in military style, to give people the impression that as leaders in society we were a willing extension of their power. We debated among ourselves various ways to avoid it. But the Kempeitai, the toughest and cruellest Japanese secret operatives, called us in and made it clear they would ensure we complied. They had the power. We couldn't possibly deal with them unless we suppressed our feelings and accepted the reality of their dominance.

GOOD DORMITORY, BAD FOOD. WE MOVE TO PRAPATAN 10

The name "Prapatan 10" would later become part of the independence movement's folklore, but for now we simply called it the 'New Asrama in Jalan Prapatan 10', inner Jakarta. It was a series of new buildings done in an old fashioned style, with a spacious backyard. A lady named Ibu Ibnu came with the new asrama, to run the kitchen, and we ran the asrama with almost no reference to the Japanese. That was a limited freedom, however. The Japanese were a formidable force. When they wished for something to be done it was done, whether we liked it or not. Suyono, Sudiharjo and Amino, who lived locally, were our new asrama managers and everything seemed to run fairly smoothly. But even they could not help the deteriorating food situation, which quickly went from fair to worse in quality with the portions getting smaller and smaller.

THE JAPANESE TRY TO PLANT A MILITARY SPY

The Japanese tried to place a soldier who understood basic Indonesian as a permanent guard in charge of us, to spy on us. He was a sergeant, although he stayed such a short time we hardly knew him. He was the object of impolite jokes in phrases he could not follow, and at night he rarely slept more than a few minutes because we had riddled his bed with lice, gathered from the kampung huts close by. These little Satans loved the sergeant's blood and bit him all through the night until finally, he couldn't tolerate it. He was not a naturally sharp fellow. But sharp enough to want a good sleep.

The sergeant soon left us, but we suffered the consequences of our biological warfare because we had been a little careless in handling the lice and some had found their way into our own beds. We had to turn out all the mattresses in the sun and clean them, which probably allayed any Japanese suspicions about the origin of the lice in the sergeant's bed and reinforced their opinions that after all, we were country bumpkins.

Our level of enthusiasm for learning was high. Prapatan 10 was a good distance from the Faculty in Jalan Salemba, so we got there by tram or bicycle, and I often ran the distance to keep fit. We had done physical training with the Japanese in Bogor so we could easily run 5 kilometres.

LIVING STANDARDS PLUNGE

While our own living standards were clearly sinking, those of the common people were declining faster, almost daily. We also saw the physical suffering of patients in the general hospital, the result of poor nutrition. By the end of the first year of the Japanese Occupation, living conditions became very poor and there was palpable fear in the air. Our people were cowed into silence, as well as hunger and exhaustion.

CADAVERS OF ROMUSHA AND THE HOMELESS PILE UP

The Anatomy Department where we worked for long hours was by 1943 flooded with bodies of the homeless and those unfortunates who later became known as *romusha*, men recruited on rosy promises to help 'Brother Japan' in their war. They were in fact slave labourers used by the army. So many had died in the streets of a combination of exhaustion, hunger and beatings that the bodies soon piled high in our department and we had to stop taking delivery. Most of these enslaved labourers were from Javanese villages and what surprised us was that so many of them had not originated from the poorest areas. That most of them were young told us the village authorities had collaborated with the Japanese and handed them over for enforced labour, a shameful chapter in our history that truly depressed and saddened us.

MY OWN HISTORY AND GOOD FORTUNE

With society plunging into the Dark Ages under the Japanese, I took flight into pondering my own relative good fortune. My parents were reasonably well positioned, and I had been educated in a Dutch school. I knew Javanese, Dutch and the Malay that would evolve into Bahasa Indonesia. My father drove a 1930 Chevrolet in an era when few people owned cars, and at school I was comfortable as a classmate with the children of Javanese nobility, especially as it was the branch of Javanese nobility that had shown themselves independent of thought and action under the Dutch rulers.

My father promised he would pay for my total education *provided I did not join the police force or the public service,* which he considered prepared personnel to reinforce the Dutch colonial administration. My adventurous streak derived from my great grandfather who took part in Prince Diponegoro's uprising in the Tuban district in 1829, today an historic site 100 kilometres northwest of Surabaya. I inherited his ambition, imagining myself as a Dr Albert Schweitzer type of doctor, travelling deep into the Borneo jungles, or New Guinea, treating primitive people and doing some big game hunting. When these daydreams faded, stark reality would envelop me and I would remember I was a captive medical student in the only medical school run under close supervision by the Japanese Imperial Army in Jakarta.

One of the most unpleasant of our duties was the enforced labour we did for the Japanese, "donating some time" as they put it. Medical students were enlisted to give their time as "honour duty" to make a landing strip in the Subang area of northwest Java, where conditions were harsh. We had poor food, a thin mattress and no bed clothing. Sunrise to sundown they worked us very hard, digging and carrying. I did not complain, for I was impressed that my colleagues had voiced my own opinion that doing this work gave us an understanding of how much worse it was for the *romusha* slaves the Japanese were using, men who worked until they could no longer stand upright and were then "set free" by the Japanese and new *romusha* put in their place until they also collapsed. We had seen these wretched figures in their last days, fossicking in rubbish tips for scraps, walking the streets almost naked, begging for scraps. They slept where they fell. Death was inevitable.

The airstrip work was a precursor to enforced military training in PETA, the Japanese inspired "National Army" designed to appeal to our national pride. But the real reason for PETA was to supply hastily trained obedient youths as cannon fodder in the front line against British or American troops in an expected invasion of Java. PETA was yet another acronym in Indonesian, for Pembela Tanah Air or Fatherland Defense Forces, whose headquarters were near the Harmoni Dance Hall, not far from today's Merdeka Palace. Harmoni had been the centre of Dutch social life in Batavia, but the dancing had ended when the Japanese arrived. The military aspect of the PETA Harmoni training was not very useful, being mostly dreary, repetitive Japanese propaganda day after day and offering us no practical military use. That was deliberate.

We soon realised that if the Japanese were truly interested in having us help them fight they would have provided better weaponry than the ancient Dutch rifles they distributed to trainees. They themselves used modern, effective weaponry. Did our boys understand it meant the Japanese did not trust us? I doubted it. The PETA boys were usually innocent young village lads with little schooling, ideal gun fodder for the Japanese to push into front lines.

Although we were vaguely formulating anti-Japanese plans, we were still in no position to act upon them. Batavia, now called Jakarta, was under a tight military hold from morning to night. Besides, our studies were taking up a lot of our thinking time and we were going along well now that those administering the practical classes were Indonesians.

JAPANESE PROPAGANDA FILMS: PREPARING TO SACRIFICE US

Almost from the start, Japanese propaganda included amateurish films directed to preparing tens of thousands of our uneducated village youths to form the front lines and take the first blows of an expected Allied landing on Java. The Japanese also tried to convince these gullible young men that sacrificing their lives for the Emperor would be heroic.

The worst of the Japanese films was a story called *Amat Heiho Jantan Indonesia* that was run hundreds of times in cinemas controlled by the Japanese. The fictional Amat was a youth in the Indonesian auxiliary who took with him an explosive and jumped into an enemy tank, blowing himself and the enemy into smithereens, but saving the lives of many deserving others who were at risk from this enemy. The filmmakers couldn't find a whitish looking enemy, so the audience is asked to guess that the enemy would have been a nasty European. We were supposed, also, to stand for the Japanese national anthem, which was a dreary, grating noise, but so many of us refused that it became impossible for the Japanese to police.

FIRST TRIP BACK TO SURABAYA, 1943

During term break in 1943, I made my first train trip back home to Surabaya to propose to my girlfriend Lily. On arrival, I met Hartadi, who was now Station Master at Pasar Turi, which along with Gubeng and Semut, was one of the big three Surabaya stations. He told me that the people had turned on an angry Japanese soldier who had become violent, claiming someone had 'stolen' his sword. Hartadi had called the Kempeitai military police who had quickly taken him away. He reported the incident to emphasize the anti-Japanese feeling in the town. After more than a year under them, the local people were starting to stand up to them, in sharp contrast to the passivity we experienced in Jakarta.

Hartadi, with his rail and port connections, had reliable intelligence on the Japanese, reporting that they held such tight control on food production that most rural villagers were suffering in a state of near starvation. He also reported that the Japanese were shipping Surabayan *romusha* labour overseas, to be used for the heavy work in fighting against the Allies on mainland Asia. They had tight control of our livestock and grain shipments going by train to port, using baton-swinging 'Train Police' to control the shipments.

The Japanese had brought in these train bullies to ensure these produce shipments went to their godowns and troop kitchens. Small traders were among the first to feel the Japanese grip, being banned from carrying the usual village produce of palm oil, duck eggs and other produce they would normally sell for a few cents profit in Surabaya. The 'Train Police' were brutal and often drew blood. Near Probolinggo the passengers had turned on one of the worst offenders in reprisal and had beaten him to death.

The Surabayans knew far more about the Occupation problems in rural Java than we did in Jakarta. Poverty in the villages set in very quickly, now that their harvests were being seized. Hunger was widespread, and through 1943–44 the people began using gunny sacks for clothing. Precious metals, jewellery and valuables were 'donated' (confiscated) and tough social controls were introduced into a village life that had previously been free and easy. The village people could hardly fail to notice how many of their young men had not returned from Japanese labour camps where they had been promised paid jobs, and were increasingly agitated when the few who did return came home as skeletal forms, hardly recognisable as family. It was clear they were being worked to death as *romusha*.

MARRIAGE: PREPARE FOR A 'MERDEKA' LIFE

I was just twenty-two years of age when I decided my life was incomplete and that I must marry Lily, the girl of my dreams, who had remained in Surabaya these past months, living with her family under a Japanese Occupation that irritated her. She was a very determined young woman, and was in some ways more advanced in her thoughts on how we were to win independence than we were in Jakarta. She said she was deeply committed to the struggle, and that I had better get used to it!

The atmosphere in Surabaya was charged, whereas in Jakarta it was docile. After marriage dates were arranged, I returned to Jakarta and immediately began trying to stir up enthusiasm for a move towards total independence. I explained the situation in Surabaya to my closest Jakarta friend, Imam 'Bok, who got excited and showed me a secret cache of firearms.

I had no idea how he had obtained them in those dangerous times but he had several weapons, claiming he got them from a highly placed, corrupt Japanese official in the propaganda department. There were three pistols, and I knew them well, for I had taken a lot of interest in guns in my school days, getting several brochures and books from the shops in Surabaya, the *Van der Linden* and *Munaut.* These publications had photos of just about every hunting rifle or pistol, complete with descriptions. My father owned a secretly obtained .32 Mauser. 'Bok's three pistols in Prapatan 10 were a Smith & Wesson .45, a Colt Woodsman .22 Target Long Rifle automatic, and a small pistol intended for women, called 'dames pistol'. We couldn't wait to fire them, so we set up a mattress and pillows to deaden the noise because the Japanese patrolled frequently in the Prapatan area. The firing went well, and I surprised friends with some sharp shooting. After the session we ambitiously claimed they were the first shots in the struggle for freedom.

MILITARY SCIENCE: MY FIRST LESSONS

I saw that the path to freedom for us would necessitate organized, military training. In term breaks in 1944, I was hungry for more knowledge of military science, so I got further secret instruction from a senior officer in the PETA auxiliary forces. His name was Abdulkadir, and he lived in Menteng where I would visit him by night. He gave me secret lessons in attack and defence tactics for small squads, up to battalion size, the use of heavy weaponry, and how to build defensive posts. I was a natural, being able to grasp formations, firepower and logistics. The PETA boys trained hard, and learned as much possible of armed combat, but while many of the others were training because they felt they owed allegiance to the Japanese 'older brothers,' and hoped one day to fight for them, the three of us from the medical school knew we were training to fight for our own freedom. I was promoted Commander of one of these Japanese units, and the two friends from medical school who were with me in special training became my deputy commanders.

SURABAYA WEDDING AND BACK TO JAKARTA, APRIL/MAY 1945

I had returned once more to Surabaya, another frightful train journey, for my wedding with Lily. I had to borrow some nice clothing for the occasion, although Lily had somehow found some wonderful material for her dress. It was a happy wedding, and being married took some of the usual pain off the return train ride back to Jakarta, where we were to somehow set up a household.

We could not go back to Prapatan 10, for that was for unmarried male medical students, so with the connivance of my friends Bok, Suwadi, Suyitno, Sugiarto and Mulyo, I was able to continue my studies while living with Lily in a room in a house close by, where the rent was surprisingly cheap. The reason being the owner feared a ghost was haunting the room so getting any rent at all was a bargain for her. Keeping a straight face (for the rent was *really* cheap) I said I believed her when she said that an evil spirit lived in the rambutan tree near the window, so I promised to be on guard.

Our Prapatan 10 group knew the Japanese were suffering somewhat, back in February 1945. Bok said there was news on the underground grapevine that the US Navy had defeated the Japanese in a major battle somewhere in the Pacific. There were other rumours that in Blitar, East Java, PETA soldiers had mutinied. All this contributed to the rising expectations and tensions within the asrama, with each member voicing his own opinion on what it really meant for the independence struggle.

The reports of Japanese setbacks in the Pacific and other areas, although far from Java, speeded up the process of political development. From the daily challenges of study, family life and leisure, we turned to political discussions, which ran into the night. We discussed our future leaders.

Around March 1945, on our way home, we suddenly dropped into Bung Hatta's home where we found him in pyjamas. He was to be our first Vice-President, a wonderful, educated Sumatran who was a counterbalance to the populist Sukarno. Dr Hatta looked rather startled at our group's sudden arrival, but said he was comforted by our show of preparedness. We were anxious to push our leaders into a more active role toward independence. Dr Hatta came out and spoke with us. We didn't learn much of practical use, but we went away mildly satisfied that we had alerted him to our readiness for action and the urgency of our demands for independence. But his language was bureaucratic in nature and deep down that disappointed us. He spoke of *Administration* while we spoke of *Revolution*. That was the perfect example of the contrasts between Jakarta and Surabaya.

The Prapatan 10 asrama was the centre of rising mutterings of rebellion within the students' quarters, with numerous meetings and fiery speeches. But the truth was we had no serious plans for action. There was a new, hopeful attitude, but not the sort of feverish activity and underground talk as in Surabaya. Jakarta was the capital, and Jakarta was where the leaders gave their speeches, so it was only natural for us to expect them to lead us, especially Sukarno, who was a very popular, influential speaker, admired because of years suffering in Dutch jails for his anti-colonial politics.

The Japanese clearly surmised that they needed to keep Jakarta under tight control because any independence movement would look naturally to the capital and the nationalist leaders. If rebellion were to break out, the Japanese could quickly get it under control, and jail or perhaps decapitate the leaders. Beheading was a common way they disposed of enemies.

I had seen that in Surabaya, the Japanese had poor intelligence, and whilst they knew the traditional nationalists and had jailed one leader, Dul Arnowo, for merely suggesting the Japanese Empire may not last forever, they were clueless about the fiery, high energy *Arek Suroboyo* boys and girls of the kampungs, on streets or in high schools and tertiary training institutions. In Jakarta, the energy among us was high, but we were under no illusion that we could buck Japanese military power. It was better for us to concentrate on developing the mood of self-assurance and self-worth, something the Japanese had tried to beat out of Indonesian society. They had imposed on our society a set of irrational rules, reinforced by rifle and bayonet and beatings, draining our self-confidence.

Moslems were told to pray to the Japanese Emperor, not Mecca, and use prayer times adjusted to Tokyo time, which was used now across all Indonesia. Sunrise in Ambon was four hours before the Sumatran dawn, but working hours were never adjusted. No arguments! It was Tokyo 'crock' time. Cyclists were forced to dismount when passing a guard post, step aside if they were on the same footpath and bow to all Japanese officers. They required us to stand for their dreadful national anthem, and herded us into cinemas to watch amateurish propaganda films that glamorized *Dai Nippon*, their term for Japan and its occupied territories. They had already drawn maps showing our eastern islands as a province of their new imperial empire, which now used oil from Balikpapan and Sumatra.

As medical students, we saw the evil underbelly of the Japanese occupation. We had inside knowledge of just how many thousands of our people they had enslaved and who were dying of overwork and starvation. Their bodies piled up in our mortuaries until we could accept no more, yet the Japanese officers in charge of us somehow expected us to find it in our hearts to treat them as they had described themselves to us in their propaganda, as a superior, invincible race, here to help us. Our saviours!

In February 1945, US and Allied bombing raids began over Surabaya, sporadically, but sufficiently evident for the Japanese censors to threaten death to anyone found listening to overseas radio broadcasts. We learned around this time from the anti-Japanese underground that Nazi Germany was failing, giving us some encouragement of change although we saw no signs of weakened Japanese resolve. Nonetheless, we now began to work much harder to form an underground movement to arm ourselves and plan an uprising against the Japanese.

SUSPICIONS OF JAPANESE ACTIONS

In Jakarta and in Surabaya we were always suspicious of Japanese actions. We thought the Japanese would suspect every trained Indonesian soldier in the PETA organisation, after the Blitar uprising, which we were now hearing details about. The Japanese had hung and decapitated numerous leaders after a show trial at Jakarta's seaside Ancol village.

My own feeling was that most PETA soldiers were in the first place chosen for their submissive attitudes and gullibility in swallowing Japanese propaganda. Nonetheless, they were in uniform, they did have weapons, mostly from the Boer War and First World War, and limited ammunition, but it was better than anything outside in society. So we were hoping that PETA Jakarta would start taking some action, and would be our most important source of arms.

PATRIOTISM AMONG STUDENTS

In general, the students in Jakarta and Surabaya had always agreed that we had to maintain communication with the 'intellectuals' and older nationalists, who were ready-made leadership material. We knew it would be left to us to do the physical work, the fighting, but we also knew we needed their management experience and their political knowledge on how to implement independence, once obtained. Splitting our forces into political or religious parties, or fighting under union banners, would soon have us defeated and back where we began, under the Dutch.

With this in mind, the Prapatan 10 group and other strong Jakarta youth groups were often called in, especially after February

1945, to meet with the *Empat Serangkai,* the 'Cluster of Four' nationalist leaders. They were Sukarno, Dr Hatta, Ki Hajar Dewantoro and Kiai Haji Mansur. 'Cluster' was common terminology for our nationalist leadership during the Japanese Occupation. We had to maintain a level of decorum during these meetings because we didn't wish to reveal our true feelings in front of the Japanese, who were there to 'oversee' the event. So we used the word "suppose" when discussing possible war outcomes, asking for example:

1. Suppose Japan is defeated before the Allies land on Java? Will we already be independent?
2. Suppose the Allied forces land before the Japanese surrender. Who is going to oppose them?
3. Suppose the Allies land after the Japanese surrender? Do they intend to bring the Dutch back?

They were unanswerable questions at our level, but the situation demanded that we determine the leaders' attitudes. We were concerned that if the Indonesian leaders were seen to be collaborating with the Japanese to declare independence, it would invite disaster upon us. We could not trust the Japanese, nor did we wish to work with them, although the leaders still felt they could not move without them. These were confusing times, in Jakarta, but as we were soon to see, in Surabaya there was absolutely no confusion about what our first, second and tertiary moves should be: *Merdeka!*

IN SURABAYA AMAT THE HERO GETS A POOR RECEPTION

Surabayans responded robustly to clumsy Japanese propaganda like *Amat Heiho Jantan Indonesia,* and so added spirit to the anti-Japanese feelings we already nursed. It was clear the youth of the city had no difficulty in keeping clear minds. We had already endured three and a half years of forced-fed Japanese propaganda by controlled radio broadcasts through loudspeakers on every crossroad, in every village market place, or public areas, and the crudely worded efforts by their soldiers to "raise the fighting spirits" of the Javanese. We plainly saw the Japanese promises for us to be within a "Greater Southeast Asia" to be hollow words.

In the early months of 1945, frequent references were made to the missing *romusha*. Whilst the villagers could not have known the percentage of *romusha* deaths (later estimated at 70%) there was by 1945 little doubt that these men were unlikely to return alive, that the initial promises made by the *romusha* hiring gangs were empty and misleading, and that the Japanese were culpable.

The youth groups, both in Jakarta and Surabaya, at least agreed with each other in concluding that all Indonesian youth, our *Pemuda,* had to oppose *any* force – Japanese, Allied, Chinese, pro-Dutch within our own ranks, Eurasians or even Arab merchants – who opposed our *Merdeka!* movement. We proposed the three points:

1. Our aim is a Free Indonesia
2. We will use arms to fight anyone who opposes a Free Indonesia
3. We will seize weapons to arm ourselves.

The only source of weapons available to us was the Japanese.

Although we were politically immature, we knew a little about fascism. The Dutch had rounded up members of the pro-German National Socialist League just before the Japanese landed. The Japanese protected these same people during their occupation, so we soon understood what that fascism meant terror, threats, massacres on a large scale, cheating, crude and some refined propaganda, corruption, and racial insults against Indonesians during the entire occupation. We knew what fascism was!

The Japanese provided a 'synthetic cohesion' among youth groups as well as the older nationalists, by their years of maltreatment. This cohesion kindled hopes that strong free Indonesian movements would finally replace the Dutch. Nothing else mattered, provided Indonesia had its independence. What *was* achieved during these long discussions during the Japanese occupation was a spreading, growing political awareness and confidence. We knew intuitively there would be bloodshed, although we were so young and inexperienced we had no idea of what it would be like. The Dutch had folded quickly to the Japanese, and the Allies never did land on Java to attack the Japanese. We had no example of what war was like. The Prapatan 10 group in May reinforced the stated aims:

1. Indonesian independence: *Merdeka*
2. Armed action against those opposing *Merdeka*
3. Indonesian youth must seize Japanese weapons

On 28 May, in Jakarta, a body for the Study of Independence Preparations met with Dr Hatta, with Sukarno attending. My older friend from Prapatan 10, Imam Slamet 'Bok, warned the Study members to prepare for Japanese tricks. We then heard Bung Sukarno would go overseas to discuss our independence. But apparently the talks did not get anywhere, with the Japanese continuing to give vague promises and speaking of a glorious future for Asia.

TIME TO RETURN HOME TO SURABAYA

By the start of August 1945 Lily, being very pregnant, felt she would be a burden to us in any fighting in Jakarta, so we agreed that I would return to Surabaya with her to see her safely home, expecting to return for the action in Jakarta. All my medical school colleagues agreed, so I said I would be back in the capital as soon as possible. We had already heard on the underground network that the Germans had unconditionally surrendered to the Allies back on May 7, which would hurt the Japanese and bring about a quicker end to the war. But all this news was blanketed in a cloak of secrecy for the Indonesian people.

It was yet another dreadful journey for her, the carriages packed, the air stifling, with many poor people standing all the way, night and day. The carriage was overcrowded, and she vomited several times. Lily was given a torrent of motherly advice from a woman who discussed every aspect of child bearing, raising children, marrying and keeping house until Lily's head ached, so I gave the old lady a sleeping pill, which worked quickly. Lily was envious, also wishing to sleep so I had to give her one too!

JAPANESE DISBAND PETA, EARLY AUGUST 1945

In early August 1945 the Japanese sprang a surprise. They called all the PETA soldiers throughout Java to parade, on the same day, and requested they leave their weapons behind so they could be "more properly stored." The PETA boys fell for this shallow deceit. To our shame, not one PETA soldier called their bluff and refused to hand in his weapon. The Japanese had chosen these malleable recruits from public service ranks or villages, obsequious boys trained to obey orders, from the Dutch and the Japanese. The Blitar uprising in East Java was the only attempt to remove the Japanese military power on Java. The Surabaya youths were busy running around town co-ordinating links with the people. Hartadi daily monitored the events in Jakarta through the personnel on the Surabaya-Jakarta-Surabaya train run, so they were fairly well informed. Jakarta, on the other hand, knew little of events in Surabaya.

THE JAPANESE SURRENDER!

With a suddenness that astounded Indonesians, the Japanese surrendered on 15 August 1945. The news, however, did not spread immediately. The Japanese delayed the announcement wherever they could, but the rumours of defeat were in the air. We had no time to organize an uprising in Jakarta and now, they had surrendered. Although the surrender was soon known to be unconditional, from 15 August to the end of August the Japanese tried to save face by keeping it secret from Indonesians and their own lower ranks, so we were well into late August before we learned they had lost the war.

To continue this abysmal avoidance of the truth, they told their senior officers that Japan had gone into a "ceasefire" and "the war would not continue." Some of us felt they had done this to avoid an outbreak of *harakiri* suicides. The Japanese in Java had surrendered to an invisible enemy! How could they have lost the war? None of them had faced fire, or even seen an American, British or Australian soldier, and they were aware that *we were aware* of this. Their strutting and bombast were now empty gestures. Their attitudes towards us went from the pretence of friendship to open hostility.

We were briefly ecstatic, expecting them to go home and leave us in peace, but that was not to be. The Japanese, after having promised to help our popular nationalist leader Sukarno move toward independence and self-rule, had failed. They had, just days before the surrender, flown our nationalist leaders to Dalat in southern Vietnam and promised a half-measure of independence to them, but had neither told Sukarno or Hatta that the Americans had dropped atomic bombs on Japan, nor that they had surrendered unconditionally. Within a week we learned these via underground sources, yet were astonished at the duplicity and face-saving excuses they had served up to Indonesians.

In Surabaya the Japanese in administrative positions now showed little interest in their work, and made obvious preparations to depart. The military compounds, on the other hand, seemed on high alert. It was still dangerous to speak about the surrender and the atom bombs. The 'secret' seemed to heighten the tensions.

THE PROCLAMATION OF INDEPENDENCE

Sukarno and Dr Hatta had been urged by Jakarta youth to proclaim independence on Friday 17 August 1945. But it was to remain a proclamation of intent only, for some months and many feared it would never be realised. The Proclamation news was broadcast briefly on Radio Jakarta, but Japanese censors successfully prevented the news from being broadcast in Surabaya for some hours. Our journalists in Jakarta, including youth leader Adam Malik, found a way to get the news to radio technicians in Radio Surabaya. The news reached us via 'illegal' channels in Antara news agency where Malik, a future vice-President, and others had subverted the system.

Radio Surabaya, under our manager Sukirman, broke the news of the Proclamation right under the noses of the Japanese censors, by having our newsreader Jakfar read the 1900 hours bulletin in Madurese, which had many familiar rhythms to Malay. The censors had no inkling of what he had done. The Madurese were the salt distributors, the *pikulan basket* traders, the refuse garbage men and general menials in the kampungs. A good proportion of them were descendants of Madurese who had lived in or close to Surabaya for centuries. They were physically taller, had darker skin tones and were generally less refined than the Javanese, but they were reliable allies and not at all fond of the Japanese.

Post Proclamation, our Jakarta leaders began meetings to form ministries, and they produced documents and ministerial lists. But the Minister for Works had no public work and the Minister for Finance had no finance. We had declared independence but had no freedom. They advised us to quickly organise the apparatus of government in Surabaya, while they in Jakarta held fiery meetings and endless conferences.

THE BRITISH HARNESS THEIR ENEMIES TO BECOME OUR ENEMIES

We thought they could sink no further in our estimation, but the Japanese had one more very nasty lesson for Indonesians. After arriving at Tanjung Priok on Saturday 15 September, the British South East Asia Command enlisted the Japanese troops, now their prisoners-of-war, to "keep the peace" in Indonesia. In other words, the Japanese continued their control over us as they had under their Occupation, to ensure the Dutch could safely return to power to rule the Netherlands East Indies. We heard reports from Bandung where Japanese troops had willingly helped the British crush the youth uprisings. Far worse news was to come from Semarang. We in Surabaya were soon to learn the Japanese seemed to delight in working with the British in killing our youths fighting for independence, in Bandung, Bogor, Cirebon and Semarang.

The Japanese, the British, and newly arrived aggressive and aggrieved Dutch troops, using tall Ambonese among them, held the real power in Jakarta, though at night the city was mutinous, with shootings and bizarre robberies. Even the popular Sukarno dared not order the people to seize weapons from the Japanese or hinder the British in their work. At public meetings the Japanese stood guard, grim-faced, shining bayonets fixed, at strategic points.

JAKARTA PASSIVE, STILL!

I had to make a quick trip back to Jakarta, but before I went my mother-in-law said to me, "you'll be back here before long." I arrived in Jakarta on August 20 and went straight to Prapatan 10. My room was still empty and my belongings undisturbed, including a sword I had hidden.

Instead of the usual rowdy greetings and the distribution of cakes, there was just the greeting and the clamouring for news from Surabaya. I told them "Arek Suroboyo sudah siap", meaning that Surabayan youths were ready to fight. But Jakarta should act now, and lead the way. I was sorry I had missed the Proclamation, but in fact, I was starting to get somewhat disappointed in Jakarta. I had imagined that Prapatan 10 would be the headquarters of some insurrection, full of youths with rifles, ready to go into action. What I found was a quiet asrama with three cars stolen from the Japanese in the yard.

We wanted facts and action, not speeches with well-rounded phrases. We wanted to take over the administration of Indonesia from the capital in Jakarta, where we had declared the Proclamation of Independence. It was time to take power from the Japanese. They had already surrendered unconditionally but were still fully armed and controlling daily events in the city. To take over, we would have had to disarm them.

THE PRAPATAN 10 PUZZLE

We were still in a muddle, all wishing for independence, but now we were wondering just who we would be fighting. The British had seconded the Japanese to keep the peace, on their behalf. If we attacked them the British could soon come down on us. The Allies had defeated the Japanese, so in theory they would have been in favour of hammering the Japanese, but the British were intent on bringing the Dutch back to power, and needed the Japanese as support troops to keep the independence movement in check. Back in March we tried riding around Jakarta looking for easy targets, Japanese from whom we could seize weapons, but found none. All our political thinking had been directed to an uprising against the Japanese in Jakarta, but that had all changed. Now, in September 1945, with the Japanese defeated, Indonesians everywhere were asking: would be we fighting the British or the Japanese? As it turned out later in Surabaya, we fought both!

MY FINAL DEPARTURE FROM JAKARTA

The Prapatan 10 student leaders then felt they had no option but to divide their duties. I was chosen to return to Surabaya for a third time to organize matters to "defend independence" (*mempertahankan kemerdekaan*). Already in mid-August they were speaking in those terms, of "defending independence."

In the train home, in what would be my last journey for a long time, I was lucky to get a corner seat near the window on a packed train. To get such a seat we had to plan cleverly by staying overnight very close to the station, then a group of us would head for the Kota station in the morning to get to the head of the queue for a ticket so that the passenger could board when the doors opened. If I had left from the Prapatan 10 asrama that morning, I might have been caught in traffic, or in previous years, be halted by air raid sirens. After getting a seat, the boys would then push my luggage through the window.

SOLEMN THOUGHTS DURING A CROWDED TRAIN JOURNEY

Everyone else in the packed train seemed preoccupied with their own thoughts. None seemed to want to discuss the Proclamation. I wondered if those around me were truly uninterested in the political events or if they were still afraid and suspicious that Japanese spies were present and would report them. I tried to convince them of the importance of our changed times, and embrace the concept of *Merdeka!* Cowed people are not easily raised to action. They had been under Japanese rule for so long now they had lost their initiative. The hunger besetting them was for nourishing food, not political philosophies.

Most of them appeared to be people who had had it hard during the Japanese years. Only a small number of people enjoyed life under the Japanese. They were the collaborators or black marketeers who operated with the tacit agreement of the Japanese. They wore good clothing, could afford new tyres for their bicycles, and produced a wad of notes when they were buying anything. Many of them were drawn by the quick profit from trading illegal items such as medicine, antibiotics, decorations, gold, jewellery, rice and flour and food. They generally worked with the corrupt Japanese, whose mafia, the *Sakura*, were among their ranks. Others were known to moonlight as informers for the secret police, the *Kempeitai*. These black marketeers faded quickly from the scene when the anti-Japanese movements began, taking their booty and escaping to distant towns or provinces and taking on a new guise with a name change, as a loyalist.

Compared to what others in the carriage were wearing, my clothing was not unusual. My shirt was made from two trouser legs from discarded trousers that had been cleverly sewn together by an expert seamstress. If we wanted anything of quality, even soap, we had to buy it on the black market at very high prices. Whatever we grumbled about we blamed on the Japanese, whether they had anything to do with it or not. By this time in Jakarta it was common for the homeless to wear gunny sacks for clothing.

Opposite me on this trip was an old woman nursing an infant

who could have been her grandchild. People packed the corridors, their faces devoid of expression. In their minds these were still treacherous times. The Japanese were still strutting around Jakarta as though they were in charge. No one had been safe from Kempeitai spies, and the feelings lingered even after surrender; people preferred to remain mute. The infant's crying brought me back from my daydreaming. I was sweating, and soot from the coal-burning locomotive was threatening to hurt my eyes, but I couldn't close the window because the air was stifling.

I hadn't brought much luggage along, just a few items of clothing in a small case and one particularly unusual item, a Samurai sword bought from Gakuto Kai swordsmanship training. I had graduated in *Kendo* (swordsmanship) only at a basic level, but the sword gave me the confidence to meet most challenges.

Despite our slightly elevated status in society as tertiary students, our suffering was almost as bad as the common people during the Japanese times, in contrast to the Dutch colonial years when students were held in high regard. We had mastered a foreign language and understood European society and Western mannerisms. It was true that the Japanese Imperial Army had easily defeated the colonial powers in Southeast Asia but their boast to being a superior race was quickly seen to be an empty claim. Their soldiers were like unthinking robots, rude and brutal, their language crude and hateful, and their administration ruthless and irrational. To educated people their propaganda was utterly banal, insulting even to villagers who had grown up with the lively sophisticated cultural exchanges emanating from oral histories or wayang shadow play and puppet theatres that carried endless instructive wisdom.

I tried to envisage what I would do upon arriving in Surabaya, but it was hard to concentrate in that hot, crowded carriage and a lot easier to daydream. For me, the train was just crawling along, going too slowly.

I planned to start my campaign by contacting old friends and relatives and, with their aid, to form new connections. The foundation of our struggle would be to align society's views to the single aspiration of *Merdeka!* Perhaps that was a little simplistic. I fell into a deep sleep, amidst the smell of sweaty bodies. The carriage air was thick with smoke from home-made tobacco, the scent of jackfruit and various other unidentifiable smells.

2

TEARING OF THE TRICOLOUR

The slow, overloaded train from Jakarta finally drew into Surabaya
with the passengers drained and weary after almost thirty hours
of discomfort. I soon found my old friend Hartadi at his strategic
post as Station Master of Pasar Turi and he secretly arranged
a telephone call back to Prapatan 10, using the railway signals
telephone connections.

I told the Prapatan 10 boys I had found plenty of independence
action in Surabaya. Hartadi had sacked some of the Eurasians
from the Railways, fearing they would undermine the cause, and
replaced them with Indonesian workers.

The Indonesian informers used by the Japanese, who had
inherited them from the Dutch and employed them in similar
ways, had been caught out again, first when the Dutch surrendered
and now when their Japanese protectors had surrendered. In
Surabaya they knew that we knew who they were and feared for
their lives, so they literally headed for the hills, south and west of
Surabaya, where they hoped they would be able to start new lives
with new names, hiding in small mountain communities to avoid
detection.

HOW TO DISARM THE JAPANESE?

Our first move was to start attacking the Japanese. The politicians were busy meeting to work out ways to form a government, but this was not the direct action we sought. The Dutch and Eurasian troops and civilians released from internment camps were now on the prowl, launching actions in many parts of the city, hoping to take back their old properties and even regain their old positions in government. We knew then we had to hurry and form a fighting corps before they had a chance to use the Allied forces to help them form a new Dutch government. The Japanese had instituted a 2100 hours night curfew, which stifled our movements, as it was meant to do. With PETA disbanded we had to devise new ways to get weapons.

According to an excited Hartadi, the youths working on the railways in Surabaya were already organising themselves into action groups to wipe out the remaining vestiges of the Japanese and Dutch informers in the system. This was an understandable move because for a long time the Eurasians and the Dutch had discriminated against native Indonesians, appointing their own to positions of power. The Japanese had continued to use the Eurasians during the occupation, despite trumpeting over Tokyo Radio in pre-war programs that Japan would help us in our quest for independence.

Although our railway workers had always had some form of a union, they had been unable to improve their conditions or make much headway against the ruling powers. The Dutch colonial administrators had realised that railways were an important part of government and private business operations. They had put in place a network of informers and also established a competing union whose membership was Dutch and Eurasian, to ensure our demands for some form of equality were frustrated. During the Japanese years the railway workers were not able to make much headway against the Japanese, who kept control of the Indonesian staff with minimum effort. Now, things were about to change.

I was finding it more difficult than I had imagined gathering new friends to engage in independence uprisings. Although I had grown up in Surabaya, I was not finding it easy to locate many of my old friends, who had apparently dispersed for work or to get away from the Japanese, so I first approached my father-in-law Maskan Sumiharjo for guidance, telling him my plans.

Maskan's advice was to start at the top, not with friends of my age. He put me in touch with the key leaders of the older generation, members of the pre-war anti-colonial movements where I soon made good progress. My first call was on Pak 'Dirman, our friendly name for Sudirman, a talented civil servant who was soon to be elected first Republican Resident, or City Administrator. I had known him since I was a child, playing in his house with his children who had been with me in the Indonesian Boy Scout movement. Pak Dirman had been a friend of my father's. As a political leader in the nationalist movement, his briefing on the situation was truly valuable, sharing the nationalists' plans to remove the Japanese. But he was adamant that the youth of Surabaya had to do the hard physical work of confronting the Japanese if we were to seize weapons from them, though he could not outline precisely how we would go about the physical attacks.

Other leaders in Surabayan society included Ruslan Wongsokusumo and Pak Sungkono, friends of my father from the older generation. Sungkono, a former Scouts and Indonesia Party member, was a high ranking PETA officer, seen by many as the logical choice to lead any military action against the Japanese. Cak' Dul Arnowo, who gave me a lot of his time, was the most senior in age of the pre-war nationalists, and was busy forming the Provincial Independence Committee, following the decision of the Jakarta Independence Committee (KNI) formed on 22 August. The East Java Independence Committee was formed on 28 August in Surabaya, just six days later, so we were moving fast. Dul Arnowo was chosen as Chairman and the sub-branch was chaired by Ruslan Wongsokusumo.

The Surabaya leadership, however, was still hoping for a lead from Jakarta, not realizing that Jakarta was still placid, under the control of the Japanese, whereas we were busy planning action.

I tried extending my network by riding around the town on a bicycle, connecting with old school friends and even members of my wrestling team from the Dutch days. Most had left school early because they could not afford to continue their studies, so they had become part of the general work force, at the lowest levels of employment. Mustopo and Harto, for example, were now mechanics at the railways, as their fathers had been before them. Members in their social and work circle had developed strong anti-Japanese sentiments that they promised would soon be translated into physical action. They wanted me to join them but I decided to hold back for the moment, wishing to reorient myself, perhaps thinking I needed to take a leadership role at a higher level.

My younger brother Suharyono, who was a middle-high school student (SMT), briefed me on an amazing event I had just missed, one that convinced me I was in the right city for *Merdeka!* action. He detailed the "the red and white movement" that had burst onto the scene on 22 August, later known as the Day of 50,000 Flags. No one was certain just where the movement began, but it was spontaneous and spread like wildfire, so very soon the footpaths, streets and kampungs and tiny *warung* shops were suddenly bedecked with small red and white paper and cloth national flags. A bullock driver had even painted a big square of red and white on his animal's belly! The breakout of national flags brought with it a feeling of excitement and expectation.

Jakarta leaders had called for the people to take over the instruments of government, so this display of flags may have been one manifestation of early planning and the flags still flying from the day were a constant reminder to us that we had to start somewhere. I realised Flag Day had reminded us of our aspirations for independence and sharpened our focus. Much later I would see Wednesday 22 August as a turning point, the day Surabayans decided to parade their independence demands openly and take on the Japanese. Meanwhile, our people *were* awakening to the challenge, staring down the Japanese. They were no longer as willing to obey as they had been in the past. But weapons, weapons! We urgently needed guns!

There was a herd instinct abroad, as elephants gathering to face an enemy. We finally launched our plans to seize weapons on Sunday 9 September, at a packed meeting of older generation leaders, former PETA soldiers and youth groups, in the National Movement Hall (*Gerakan Nasional Indonesia*), where there was a unanimous vote to form a People's Security Corps (BKR).

The GNI hall was the pride of the Surabayan people, who had built it with volunteer labour and donated materials, the muscle work being provided by the younger men, while the materials came from scouring the town and public donations. The greatest financial contribution had come from our well-known Dr Sutomo (Pak Tom) the chairman of the Parindra Party, or *Greater Indonesia Party,* the biggest of the nationalist parties of the time, founded in 1935. The historic hall embodied the spirit of commonality (*kegotongroyongan*) of the people. Students, workers, employees, and whoever else wished to participate worked Sundays or any time they were free. I recall carting stones for the foundation with a few other schoolboys, several years earlier.

During the GNI Hall meeting, I joined one of the People's Defence Units. I felt I should join a unit that could best use my military training, and while not wishing to be dogmatic about it, I was looking for a leadership role where strategic thinking was required, especially in the early phases of what was going to be a monumental challenge in getting weapons and removing the Japanese, let alone hold off a return of the Dutch Colonial rule.

THE KALIASIN BKR: A NURSERY FOR YOUNG REVOLUTIONARIES

There was a feeling of Indonesian ownership. We began to believe in...our future as young leaders in an independent Republic of Indonesia.

At the GNI Hall meeting I chose to join the Kaliasin units of the Peoples Security Force (BKR Kota) because it was an inner-city, well-located unit where I could channel my energies more efficiently. We were in the heart of the CDB, on the only main road to the north of town, and occupied an old Dutch-built, solid structure whose walls were perhaps once white and whose interior rooms were large, with high ceilings. A wide veranda supported by massive columns, faced a spacious front yard where vehicles had easy access through two impressive, large gates. When the first of us moved in we were as excited as children, planning the layout, where the offices would be, the parking for vehicles we didn't yet have and kitchens we would soon need filled. There was a feeling of *Indonesian* ownership. We began to believe in ourselves, seeing our future as young leaders in an independent Republic of Indonesia.

LOCATING THE HQ OF OUR CBD PEOPLES SECURITY FORCE

The most important factor was our proximity to the surrounding densely populated kampungs. One of my primary strategies was to ensure we could draw upon their population for recruits and logistical support for food and labour. These were kampung people who deserved far more freedom and better conditions than they experienced during Dutch rule, and especially the Japanese occupation years. It was mutually beneficial. We would guide and inspire the kampung people and in return they would provide the valuable fighting forces to support our command.

The process of founding the unit there seemed a natural reflection of the dynamics at the time, where a central position allowed us to concentrate our forces. Although we had not yet arranged guard or watch duties, or a functioning kitchen, matters from the start seemed to run smoothly. Night and day the building was busy with *pemudas* (young men and women) coming and going, and very soon the married women in the surrounding kampungs had set up a communal kitchen for us, contributing equipment and food, and fussing over us as children showing us how it was done.

I was the only tertiary student in the BKR City unit. The other tertiary students, from Surabaya's Faculty of Dentistry, were in the BKR East Java unit headed by the colourful Dr Mustopo; with its HQ in the business district in the old Amsterdam Trading

Association building (HVA: *Handels Vereeniging Amsterdam*).Their primary functions were political, not military.

Many of Dr Mustopo's students were trained in espionage, and at a crucial time placed as spies in the Yamato Hotel (the former Oranje luxury hotel, now the Majapahit), where they learned to tap telephones and follow the drift of whispered conversations in Dutch and English. The hotel had been world famous during the Dutch times, being a social centre for Europeans. Built in 1911, it was one of the great showpieces of luxurious colonial living in the Indies. Founder Lucas Martin Sarkies, who married a Dutch socialite, had named the hotel for the Dutch Royal Family. The Japanese senior officers used the hotel and its luxurious surrounds, and although they changed the name to the *Hoteru Yamato*, Surabayans doggedly stuck to using *Oranje*. International celebrities, including Charlie Chaplin, attended the opening of a new art-deco foyer in 1936. White uniformed staff, three to a guest, doormen with braid and sashes, and five meter long *rijsttafel* heaped with the finest foods, adorned postcards sent worldwide by fortunate travelers advertising their good luck in being accepted into the Sarkies Oranje society. Dr Mustopo's intelligence operators were stationed in this famous foyer and in the famous dining rooms, noting the arrival of Dutch, British and other European officials whose central duties were to organize the release and care of civilians imprisoned by the Japanese.

THE BRITISH ARRIVE IN TANJUNG PRIOK, JAKARTA

Mountbatten's British South East Asia Command forces had arrived in Indonesia on the HMS *Cumberland* at Tanjung Priok in Jakarta on Saturday 15 September, a week after the GNI meeting in Surabaya that put in place our Peoples Security organisation. The British in Jakarta were starting the job of disarming the Japanese for repatriation and making safe prisoners of war being released from Japanese camps. They were under orders to await the Dutch leaders who were arriving from Australia where they had seen out the war. The Dutch intended to pick up where they had left off after being overrun by the Japanese, as rulers of the Netherlands East Indies.

Because the Dutch Army had been defeated and depleted by the Japanese, the British-Indian Army had inherited the responsibility of bringing the Dutch back, although several Dutch officers had been seconded to help them. Thus it was a combination of Dutch and British officers who had been parachuted into Surabaya to prepare the way for a British landing. They were billeted at the Yamato/Oranje Hotel. We were immediately on guard.

At the Oranje, the staff included those dentistry students, posing as menial hotel staff and dining room waiters, whose duties were to listen in on conversations and tap the telephones of the Japanese and European officers, especially those Dutchmen who seemed to be preparing for a Dutch return. The students would then pass on the information to "passers-by" outside.

In this way, they first heard whispers of Dutch intentions to raise a Dutch flag over the hotel. The staff alerted their contacts outside, which led to the September 19 "flag tearing incident," later designated by historians as the start of the physical revolution. But for now, I was just keeping an eye on the Yamato because I had many other duties establishing the Kaliasan HQ.

Two old school friends, Ronokusumo and Ronopradopo, and other former PETA soldiers had turned up at Kaliasin, to my delight and surprise. Our highest privilege was to have Dul Arnowo, the most senior of pre-war nationalist leaders come in as our patron. He was chairman of the KNI Independence Committee, and the slightly younger Abdul Wahab, also a well-known senior activist who was a fearless fighter. He rather enjoyed the soubriquet of 'Limpy Wahab' after being wounded and carted off to hospital during combat against the Kempeitai.

Asmania, Abdul Wahab's wife, was also an old friend of mine from my scouting days. She was actually a member of another unit but saw Kaliasin as the ideal place to devise ways to harness the peoples' power, and so used it as a second home. Her English was good, so we both drew up placards in English and those slogans found their way onto walls and widely distributed leaflets, some of which are seen in old black and white file photographs of these events. But putting up placards and signs didn't satisfy me. More than that, I wanted to tear down signs, all signs and traces of the Japanese power that everywhere surrounded us in Surabaya.

Because the PETA had mutinied against the Japanese in Blitar, four hours south of us in East Java, I thought the former PETA soldiers in the BKR would have action plans. But they were bereft of ideas. I suspect they had felt inadequate and were suffering a loss of confidence after the failure of the mutiny and had now preferred to wait for others to lead. There had been widespread condemnation of them for humbly handing over their weapons to the Japanese and they were naturally dispirited. I vowed to give them back their confidence, and rather soon. Their eyes would light up and their backs stiffen if they got hold of some Japanese Light Machine Guns, which would make for a change from the Boer War single shot rifles the Japanese had given them.

TAKING ADVANTAGE OF JAPANESE FACE-SAVING VULNERABILITIES

Were we still to await directions from Jakarta where our leaders were meeting with the Allies? We were now able to listen to overseas broadcasts and unless we didn't follow the English well it appeared to us that this was high time we got moving. But to our astonishment and anger, the Japanese took to the air with new instructions, ordering all radios destroyed. They were nominally still in charge and had access to Radio Surabaya.

We read it as their last desperate measure to prevent Surabayans from knowing the full extent of Japanese defeat. Most of us knew anyway, but it was a valuable insight into their abysmal reach into our society that they thought us uninformed. If they were so intent on face-saving censorship, even among their own ranks, we could use that psychology to isolate one of their compounds and seize weapons, relying on them delaying the disastrous news to avoid the "infection of defeat" spreading to other compounds.

No one in Surabaya took any notice of the warning on radios, reading it as the sort of Japanese psychological warfare that no longer had currency. There were other incidents in Surabaya to call on our immediate attention. Bloody fighting had begun between our organisations and the Dutch soldiers and civilian men who had managed to get out of Japanese internment camps. They were forcing their way back into properties and businesses our youths had occupied. We claimed right of possession by dint of the Proclamation of Independence on 17 August and fully intended to stay. Our people especially took over the garages and truck and car centres once owned by the Dutch but used by the Japanese during the occupation, for they would be important to our anti-Japanese operations.

AFFIRMING REPUBLICAN POWER IN SURABAYA AND RURAL EAST JAVA

On Monday 3 September Pak Sudirman, the former chairman of Parindra party, was elected as our first Republican Resident, or City Administrator. His appointment was announced that evening, along with a series of printed instructions to be distributed to administrators in the Republic's rural strongholds of Sidoarjo, Mojokerto, Jombang and Lamongan. The instructions read as follows:

- All those opposing the Republic of Indonesia shall be severely dealt with.

- No other flag but the Indonesian flag is to be flown, anywhere.

- Those responsible for public law and order shall strictly maintain it.

- Those opposing any of the above shall be severely dealt with.

- All public works and government administration shall continue as normal, until otherwise notified.

- To every person we instruct you to carry out your daily duties in a calm, efficient and disciplined manner.

- To all working groups and gatherings we instruct you to continue working with a family spirit, mutually cooperating to maintain security and calm for the general public.

Village and town chiefs were ordered to ensure security and all business people were ordered to continue working in a "convivial, cooperative atmosphere to safeguard the security and the welfare of the people."

THE FIRST SPARK OF OUR FIERY RAGE

The Surabaya Kempeitai, by then under British orders from Jakarta, tried desperately once more to keep control, announcing they were still in charge, and ordering the people of Surabaya to obey their orders.

But their power was gone. The people not only ignored the announcements, they came out into the streets with enraged force. The Kempeitai had posted copies of their flyers all over town, but as fast as they went up, the people angrily tore them down, in front of the astonished staff. The 22 August Flag Day had brought out subterranean, nationalist passions our people had long suppressed. They were channelling their fury at the Kempei' but I saw this as an ominous, broader phenomenon, the first spark of serious, fiery rebellious rage that bluntly sought bloodshed.

From that moment the political situation rapidly quickened pace, the atmosphere became heated, and we felt in the air that very soon the people's feeling would reach a climax and there would be an outbreak of bloody, dizzying violence against the Japanese or the Dutch. The freeing of the Dutch and Eurasians from internment camps was a source of discontent, not because they had been freed but because of their attitudes toward us. The former internees, despite suffering cruelly at the hands of the Japanese, now showed contempt for native Indonesian people, so many of whom had comforted them while they were confined.

They had no interest in us winning our independence now they had regained their former confidence and wished to rule, with us as their servants. They were certain, and said it often, that as soon as the British troops arrived the Dutch would regain their former properties and positions in the colonial system.

Given that we were all subjected to the Japanese military occupation, it was regrettable that the Dutch and Eurasians had now resumed antagonistic views of superiority and it was, as I had feared, the spark that caused the first major outbreak of mortal combat. The youths and the Dutch went head on into street fighting that quickly degenerated into deadly brawls. I was at our Kaliasin Peoples Security Force (BKR) when the first seriously wounded were brought to us for first aid and we were told of many others killed. This put our BKR boys into fighting mode. They began to sharpen bamboo and other spears, and arm themselves with long *parang* swords, made by sharpening flat steel strips such as car springs, and traditional *kris* knives.

At that juncture none of us had access to firearms. We were headed into a revolution whose elements were our new political demands, economics, psychology, ethnicity and culture, all deeply rooted in our history of the last century.

THE DUTCH STRIKE BACK

Former Dutch and Eurasian residents of Surabaya interned by the Japanese now hit back, some armed with Dutch military knives. They were adamant they would take their pre-war properties back from us, and from Yamato (Oranje) Hotel intelligence we knew they were getting moral and perhaps material support from the anti-Republican staffers of NICA (Netherlands Indies Civil Administration) who had recently arrived in Jakarta.

I was providing all this intelligence to my Jakarta colleagues, using the secret line Hartadi provided for me at his strategic post at Pasar Turi station, but Prapatan 10 had no news to offer us. It was all happening in Surabaya. Hartadi also was on the move. By mid-September he was well along in the culling process to remove known Japanese and Dutch informers from the Railways and was now in a position of strength.

This was a period of *preparation for revolution*. I spoke openly about it to Ronokusumo and Ronopradopo, both of whom I'd known since our kindergarten days, but they too were afraid to openly challenge the entire Japanese system since the failure in Blitar in February. A lot of my PETA friends were now in civvies, and less aggressive.

In Kaliasin I had time to think over the Jakarta situation. We had to assume Blitar was a lost cause. All Jakartans were familiar with the grisly end to the Blitar story, which began on 14 February 1945 as a mutiny by PETA soldiers blaming the Japanese for starving the local population and behaving with inhuman brutality. The Japanese had arrested 52 young soldiers, jailed and tortured them in prisons before holding show trials in Jakarta on Monday 16 April. Many of the 46 sentenced to long jail terms had actually died in prison from their injuries. Six 'leaders' were beheaded by sword at Ancol Beach, a resort area just north of Jakarta's CBD. Blitar PETA leader Supriyadi, who hoped also to seize the Malang radio station and broadcast an appeal for a general PETA uprising was never seen again, presumed killed by the Japanese.

Surabayan PETA members were not directly involved, but in the weeks after Blitar the Japanese had constantly spied on the city's PETA leader, Commander Sungkono, forcing him to move warily for it was clear the Japanese regarded him and his Surabaya units as untrustworthy. The Japanese were right in their assumptions. Colonel Sungkono was a natural leader and obvious choice for leadership in a revolutionary force.

THE KILLING BEGINS

They set out to kill the Dutch and Eurasians on the streets or wherever they could be found parading anti-Republican views, beating them to pulp and stabbing them to death on the streets...far beyond punching and bruising.

The next bloodletting was a few days later. We looked up to see a

British military Dakota flying over the city, dropping thousands of leaflets bearing a picture of Queen Wilhelmina and the tricolour Dutch flag. The leaflets fluttered slowly to the ground, spreading far and wide, some drifting out to sea on the winds, others falling into rice fields, but most dropping into the heavily populated kampungs. The leaflets' naive message to the people was that very soon the Dutch and Allied forces would come to Surabaya to accept the Japanese surrender, and the people of Surabaya would once more have 'their government' back. The Dutch were certain we would welcome them back warmly as our protective saviours.

The expectation of a warm welcome was proof to us of abysmally poor British and Dutch intelligence. At ground level they seemed to correctly sense the Japanese were tolerant of their activities in urging Dutch and Eurasian activists to form small groups and go into street actions against us. But our youths were anxious to get moving as vanguard fighters for a new Republican government in Surabaya that we had declared on September 3, and we had overwhelming numbers in our favour.

Now that the radio waves were open to us and we had removed the bars and seals the Japanese had put on our radios, we could hear overseas news broadcasts and knew where we stood. When the Japanese ordered us not to listen to the radio news about the Proclamation, or war news, it was just their wishful thinking.

Consequently, when the British dropped the pro-Dutch leaflets, the people became enraged, and immediately tore up the leaflets and went on a killing spree. They set out to kill the Dutch and Eurasians on the streets or wherever they could be found parading their anti-Republican views, beating them to pulp and stabbing them in violent attacks that went far beyond any of the previous clashes. It was a spontaneous outburst, the numbers in attack growing by the minute wherever a fight began. Of course the Dutch and Eurasians hit back. When the Dutch on the streets were killed the crowds searched for more in hiding. Battered and bloodied bodies were spread around the inner city streets that had once been elegant shopping centers. This was a prelude to open warfare.

Most of those killed in this round of fighting were Dutch who had come straight from Japanese prison camps and gone to their former homes or places of work, expecting the properties to be returned to them. Our youths had refused point blank, saying they were now the properties of the Republic, and the Proclamation of Independence was their authority. They had moved into workshops and auto and truck garages formerly owned by the Dutch, but managed by the Japanese.

THE TEARING OF THE DUTCH FLAG

On Wednesday September 19, as I was seated comfortably in the Kaliasin Security headquarters chatting with Ronokusumo and Cak Dul Arnowo in the high-ceilinged room, a group of younger boys came dashing in, telling us that an important Dutch person had been killed at the Oranje Hotel. An angry mob had surrounded the building, which was a sanctuary for foreign legations including the International Red Cross, now based in Surabaya for humanitarian purposes. The hotel was in Jalan Tunjungan, an elite area where wealthy Dutch families shopped. Before the war, the road was lined with shops carrying the most expensive items in emporia such as Whiteway, a Scottish department store with many branches across Asia, Aurora, Begeer van Kempen en Vos, L'Auto and others in the top bracket.

The Dental School students had overheard the Dutch in Room 33, planning to raise the Dutch flag as gesture of confidence, the first open declaration of a call to arms for the thousands of Dutch civilians and soldiers from Japanese prison camps. They would stage a march around the CBD as a show of anti-Republican strength.

But after the flag had been raised, the youths outside who had been forewarned, helped a high school student named Kusno shinny up the flagpole and tear the Dutch flag down. Once down, he and others tore the blue section from the Dutch tricolor, raising it again as the red and white Indonesian national flag. The crowd, growing by the minute, wildly applauded Kusno's feat and called for Dutch blood. Several boys then went into the lobby and confronted the Dutch group, headed by a former, prominent Master of Law and businessman, a W. V. Ch. Ploegman who during his anti-Republican outbursts, was killed after firing several shots into the ceiling. A fight ensued, involving pistols, knives, swords and clubs and a bicycle swung as a weapon.

We dashed over there, the Oranje being not far from us in Tunjungan. It was a bright, hot day, and the heat seemed to further fuel the emotions of the boys who were out in force from the inner city kampungs of Genteng, Embong Malang, Kedung Doro, Ketandan and Blauran, armed with anything they could get their hands, and shouting, "Kill the Dutch and traitors!" I saw a boy, who could not have been more than twelve years old, shouting, "I want to see Dutch blood!" The tearing of the flag had turned into a savage affair.

After the killings there was a standoff, and tempers cooled. The foreign guests, including Red Cross staff and British officers sent to supervise the release and welfare of the internees, were bystanders, and their neutrality probably saved the hotel lobby from further destruction. Not a single Dutchman ventured out from the Hotel or the Hellendorn restaurant next door where other foreign guests were gathered. I noted that none of the Japanese guards whose duty it was to keep the Oranje secure dared to intervene.

The following day, Thursday 20 September, Ruslan Abdulgani, on orders from the leaders of the independence movement in Surabaya, went to room 33 in the Oranje. Standing in the doorway and speaking in fluent Dutch, he told the conspirators their lives would be at risk if they dared anything as stupid as raising a Dutch flag in Surabaya, ever again.

(Ruslan later headed several ministries in the first of President Sukarno's administrations (1950-1965) and was Indonesia's Ambassador to the United Nations, under President Suharto. As for Kusno, the schoolboy who climbed the mast to tear down the flag, that was his last foray into violence. He later graduated in law and worked in the Department of Internal Affairs, before retiring to live on a pension until he died, around 1985.)

Some days after the flag tearing, we had confirmation that the Dutch had planned their show of strength on that day as a balance to a massively successful meeting called by our nationalist leader Sukarno, who addressed several hundred thousand loyal followers in Jakarta's Medan Gambir (now Merdeka Square) in defiance of a Japanese ban on public meetings. Japanese guards were posted around the huge audience but were not needed. Sukarno's speech was a demonstration of his popularity. The speech contained no threats, but revealed to the Japanese, the British and the Dutch who controlled the city, that Sukarno's authority was absolute.

Late in the evening, after the flag incident, Bung Wahab came around to the Kaliasin headquarters and suggested we drive around the town at night and survey the town. We really wanted some air and some time to think about the serious ramifications of the Ploegman killing, which by the next day would be discussed widely and perhaps used as an excuse for pre-emptive action against us. We were not quite ready. The previous killings were ugly street fights between our boys and Dutch civilians. The Oranje Hotel opposition was a serious, top-level attempt to reinstate the Dutch and the men involved had the power to raise a small army.

After visiting several branch encampments of the People's Security Corps (BKR) in the Baliwerti, Temban, Peneleh, Sambongan (the former Dutch Army barracks) and Gubeng areas, we knew our fears were well founded. The next day the flag incident had triggered serious repercussions, with youth groups planning more serious action after getting weapons. This would see tens of thousands of kampung street fighters out looking for a fight—Surabaya was Indonesia's biggest city in those days—and that was a concern as we needed more time to discipline them, not to mention seize sufficient weapons for them to use in our planned takeover of the city.

They didn't have the sort of military training or discipline that I had experienced under the Japanese, but they had a fighting spirit and clear concepts of what they wanted and that was to defend their one-month-old Republic of Indonesia. Formalities and law as yet played no part in their ranks. All they required was devotion to the Republican cause and every member did whatever they could in whatever role they chose. In that atmosphere, to our delight and surprise, many natural leaders came to the fore, and the senior leaders were able to dampen their furies somewhat, without curbing their initiative.

TAMBAKSARI MASS MEETING

The formation of the BKR Security Force gave structure to the freedom movement, allowing us to organise ourselves into smaller action units of around 400 personnel in various strategic locations. The successful staging of the *Rapat Raksasa* (Giant/ Mass Meeting) at Tambaksari Square on Sunday afternoon, 23 September, was proof of our new organizational strength.

In 1945 Tambaksari was a broad expanse on the edge of town—these days it is a football stadium. Surrounding it was a major housing complex built for middle-ranking public servants, built by the City Council in the Dutch times, and further out were broad, unkempt areas where tall trees still grew, a favourite playground for imaginative children. The Tambaksari meeting was widely advertised over Radio Surabaya, with leaflets and posters and information in all branches of the BKR and the PRI (Indonesia Youth) that had been formed two days earlier 21 September. Small wonder that more than 100,000 came to Tambaksari that day; I was one of them, right up front. I didn't want to miss a word.

Surabaya Radio's role was very important. We had seized the station from the Japanese on 22 August and renamed it RRI, Radio Republic Indonesia. We had also taken over the *Suara Asia* (Voice of Asia) daily newspaper from the Japanese and relaunched it as *Suara Rakyat* (People's Voice) and the two media combined helped us disseminate our message to the people. On Sunday 16 September two truckloads of Japanese soldiers arrived at RRI and attempted to forcibly seize one of the transmitters, but the staff and men from the nearby kampung Embong successfully fought them off.

The day before the attempted seizure of the transmitter some RAPWI (Repatriation of Allied Prisoners-of-War) staff had approached the station in Embong Malang requesting the use of a trained telegraphist, to be seconded to them. RRI manager Sukirman said he was willing to help, but wished to know more details. Sukirman, who understood Dutch, followed the RAPWI group back to their headquarters in Hotel Oranje, where he saw them meeting with Dutch personnel as well as English RAPWI officers. His suspicions were further aroused when he saw the former Japanese technician Takeuchi with them and he drew the obvious conclusion that Takeuchi was helping the Dutch get their hands on the transmitter.

Radio Surabaya staff had also seized scores of loudspeakers – the hated "speaking trees" the Japanese used to bombard us night and day with amateurish propaganda telling us how wise and clever the Japanese Older Brothers were – and turned them to good use for our own nationalist cause. RRI had first used the speakers to announce a public meeting to raise nationalist spirits, on open ground not far from Pasar Turi station, on Monday 17 September. The meeting was a big success, but clearly a much bigger ground was needed, so the bigger Tambaksari ground was chosen.

RRI by 23 September had increased the number of loudspeakers by repairing damaged units, so by the Sunday of the Tambaksari gathering the system was working almost citywide. Tambaksari was the greatest open-air congregation of people since before the Japanese occupation and was a credit to the youth forces and our pursuit of independence, and a big step towards preventing a return of the Dutch. The sea of people who had endured the inequities of the colonial system, then suffered even more under the repressive Japanese military rule, demonstrated renewed spirit to rid themselves of both powers and uphold the August 17 Proclamation.

In my position upfront, and wearing my Samurai sword, I almost stood against the speakers' platform. There were many fiery, uplifting speeches made to a receptive audience. We were *ready for a fight.*

Abdul Wahab, chairman of the BKR Surabaya, spoke tough: "If necessary, I will become a living bomb to destroy the enemy," perhaps imitating the dare-to-die Japanese kamikaze bombers in the Pacific. He used it as a metaphor, for I couldn't imagine him strapping a mine to himself and jumping into an enemy tank, but it sure sounded impressive.

Speakers told the crowd the youth groups must now take strong action. Our Proclamation clearly called on us to seize all instruments of power from the Japanese. Force would be met with force, said the speakers, who included Kusnadi, a youth leader from Surabaya City.

The spirit and power of the meeting permeated Surabaya, overflowing into a meeting later that evening of the Generation of Indonesian Youth (AMI), chaired by Ruslan Abdulgani, in the National Hall in Bubutan. The AMI had been formed with the blessing of the Japanese who had hoped to use the movement for their own purposes. The membership then comprised former members of groups banned by the Dutch. But the majority of AMI members now turned on the Japanese and voted that evening to seize power and weapons and integrate the AMI with a left-wing group formed two days earlier, which was headed by a student named Sumarsono.

Over the next days, with the feelings of Tambaksari still simmering, Bung Wahab and I sat down to plan how we could seize weapons from any of the several well-guarded Japanese armouries. Wahab had just one pistol, from the early days of the Japanese occupation, but it had never been fired.

The mood in the city was expectant, but one also of frustration, because the Japanese and the British, who would soon arrive, had at their call thousands of well-trained soldiers with the latest modern weapons, jeeps, tanks and fighter planes, and firepower sufficient to kill hundreds of us in an afternoon. We needed to counterbalance these forces with our own weapons, and hurriedly train boys to use them. Wahab and I decided to take the initiative on weapons seizure, but we were still unsure where to start.

We needed some peace to reflect on our position, so we called a driver and had him drive us slowly around the old town in a jeep, on an old-fashioned ride down memory lane. We drove around the city's former elegant and fashionable boulevards, taking the circuit that in the early colonial years was called *puter Kayoon*, the "puter" being the verb "to promenade". Families of all levels used to take to the cool evening air in elegant horse-drawn carriages, the ladies and their chaperoned daughters on show, all decked out in their finery, and passengers enjoying the welcome cool.

There had been modern emporia whose high fashions were on display in windows that stayed lit during the night, four huge bookstores stocked with the finest illustrated volumes in several European and Asian languages and art studios laden with paintings and sculptures and Indies crafts. The Simpang Club was a luxurious venue where tennis, billiards, dancing and card nights were featured. The Simpang and Oranje Hotel staff wore great uniforms using Javanese headdress and colorful diagonal sashes. A special treat for any Surabayan family was to go to the Oranje for their famous Sunday *rijsttafels,* long rice table buffets with 26 dishes.

The Surabaya I knew growing up was a modern port city catering for ships and crews from every continent, with efficient tramways, trains with clean carriages and reliable timetables. The buildings glowed from whitewashed walls and monuments, solid banks, offices, modern automobiles, luxury hotels and prestige shopping districts. Tunjungan Boulevard had fashionable bars and theatres and Tjioda, the first Japanese department store in Surabaya that also lit its display windows at night.

All that was lost when the Japanese Army marched in, as though a whole district had faded away, losing its colour and character like a burnt photograph. The Japanese had taken us back to the Dark Ages, and now the Dutch seemed determined to prevent us from winning our independence. We would all be losers. The *puter Kayoon* rides would be lost to us forever.

The next morning, the weapons raids began. That delightful evening ride was to be the last of inner city, imitative colonial life. I dreamed horrid dreams that these streets would soon be strewn with bodies and literally drenched in blood, the elegant shops and mansions bombed to rubble, and the stench of explosives and colours of death permeate the historic boulevards. My lively imagination had the dreaded habit of accurately foretelling the dark future of my lovely town. The wanton, senseless destruction of my town would certainly come. Chance favours the prepared, whether the preparation is in the form of nightmares or dull hard work.

3

ARMS RAID AT DON BOSCO

SEIZING WEAPONS

Our headquarters had intelligence that the British would be landing in Surabaya within a few days. They would disarm the Japanese and clean out the armouries to ensure we could not get weapons; no doubt, they were already rearming the Royal Netherlands East Indies Army (*Koninklijk Nederlands Indisch Leger*, KNIL) forces. We had to act quickly.

At dusk on Wednesday, September 26, we made our first raid. Four members of our Kaliasin Peoples Security Unit and I were among a big, noisy crowd that encircled, then broke into the Don Bosco Japanese military compound and armoury. This military post was a former convent in the heart of the Sawahan district, surrounded by densely populated kampungs. Hundreds of young men from the kampungs flooded into the compound, shaking the tall fence surrounding the compound. Among them I noticed two men using a portable loudspeaker trying to prevent the crowd from breaking down the fence. They were endangering our actions, but I was too far away to stop them, and simply cursed them. I then recognised the first one was as a former PETA officer, Mohammad, and the young speaker as Sutomo, who would later be a national hero as "Surabaya's Bung Tomo." They were urging us to hold back at a time when we desperately needed weapons! But my small squad from Kaliasin ignored their calls and used the opportunity to penetrate deeper into the compound, to a section of the building housing long benches. We came face to face with Japanese troops who were lined up, standing to attention, as if they were on guard. After our first shock, we awaited their reaction. Would they shoot? It seemed not. They were stiffly disciplined, showing no reaction whatsoever to our arrival, and made no move toward us as we approached the benches on which lay neatly arranged pistols and Japanese Arisaka carbines.

Along the wall lines of neatly arranged weapons hung from racks, as if awaiting inspection. There appeared to be more rooms similarly equipped; we were seeing just a small section of the main building. What was most surprising was the attitude of the soldiers themselves. They were silent, looking unperturbed at what was unfolding. I realised, from my experience in military training with the Japanese in Bogor and Jakarta that Japanese soldiers only moved when ordered. Had they been ordered to remain passive? Meanwhile, the crowd outside became nervous, unsure of our fate, and equally unsure of whether the Japanese would open fire on them.

In my heart of hearts I was silently cursing Bung Tomo and Muhammad for demanding the crowd withdraw. Only later did I try to understand what I considered a cowardly stance. They had both worked directly for the Japanese during the war years, and were trained to follow orders or await further Japanese instructions. They had taken it upon themselves to 'broadcast' Japanese policy, but in fact were out of step with the times. Bung Tomo would later make up for this serious mistake, when operating his Rebel Radio Station.

Inside the Don Bosco Compound, and on seeing the weapons so neatly arranged as though they had been left for us, I couldn't hold back, taking a Colt automatic with an extra clip and its holster, and a short-butt carbine off a rack, and my squad followed suit, seizing weapons for themselves. The Japanese had stored the ammunition separately, but that was of little importance, for I could get plenty of it later.

As we were leaving, the Japanese soldiers remained unmoved, standing at attention and pretending not to notice us. Carrying the weapons, we moved away from them as calmly as we could, still fearing a bullet in the back, treading slowly away from the building, then the yard, and finally, into the open street, and back to Kaliasin. I didn't care at that time what the others in the crowd were doing; it was more important to me that we had seized valuable weapons. But I soon heard that after seeing us leave with guns, the others followed in our footsteps. The next morning we heard that the boys from the kampungs returned again. On Thursday afternoon, 27 September, they overran the entire Don Bosco compound and seized all the armoury's stored weapons, with the Japanese commander, Major Hashimoto, apparently just standing by in sheer disbelief.

To forestall any possible future reprisals from the remaining Japanese, and especially the powerful Kempeitai, our People's Defence units circulated a news bulletin saying that there had been 'discussions' between the people and the Don Bosco Japanese Commander. By then most of our young BKR Kaliasin street fighters were armed, and what thrilled us even more was that the second raid had also yielded boxes of ammunition.

During that day a lot of single-fire shooting and some rare automatic firing was heard as the newly armed youths were trying out their new weapons. In the Kedungdoro kampung near my in-laws' house the boys tested their hand grenades by dropping them into wells. The explosions sounded like the firecrackers we heard on Idul Fitri holidays before the Japanese years.

GUNUNGSARI ARMOURY FALLS

Following quickly on from the 27 September raid on Don Bosco, word spread fast. Soon, all known Japanese armouries, vehicle depots and war materials stores were targeted. Street fighters from People's Security units used massing tactics to get what they wanted, a good example being the targeting of the *Kohara Butai* Japanese compound in Gunungsari on September 28, where they forced the commander to hand over the entire armoury. Hundreds of rifles, grenades and machine guns fell into our hands. That successful raid was quickly followed by another raid on the Lindeteves compound in town, which the Japanese had used as a vehicle repair shop. The boys from surrounding kampungs got help from inside, from the mechanics who used to work for the Japanese. Using the same massing tactics to overpower the Japanese, we took away light tanks, armoured cars, jeeps and various cannon and anti-aircraft guns. Two tanks were in working order, the first ones for the Republic. None of us had ever driven or been inside a tank.

Our arms seizures were now gathering pace, and while we needed organizational help, we were at least focused on the threats ahead of us. The Dutch were adamant they would return to power. Their radio propaganda on overseas broadcasts gave listeners the impression that matters in the Netherlands East Indies – the expression 'Indonesia' was not used – would soon be normalized. Senior Dutch East Indies administrators, who had safely seen out the war in Australia, were briefing the officers within the British South East Asia Command in Singapore and Batavia (Jakarta) and had convinced them the independence movement was irrelevant and any resistance would soon be quelled. We had arrested a Dutch Naval Captain, Huyer, who had been parachuted in on a reconnaissance mission, to pave the way for what he admitted was going to be a large-scale landing of Allied troops, so we knew we were headed for a major conflict.

The Dutch were still reliant on British military might. They were still unable to reform the KNIL Indies Army whose soldiers had been interned by the Japanese, and the Dutch European forces had not yet arrived. The few Dutch present in Jakarta, under British protection, had underestimated the strength and spirit of the Surabayans, judging them by the more placidly tempered Indonesians they were dealing with in Jakarta. The colonials among them, those brought up in other parts of Java or the islands, had always known Javanese to be pliant and submissive, not in the least militant. In forming policy they had mistakenly grouped the anti-feudal and anti-colonial Surabayans with Javanese of the royal court circles of Central Java, whereas those Dutch with Surabayan experience knew there was a big difference. But they were not the personnel advising the British.

So successful were our weapons raids in late September that I took time out to ring my colleagues in Prapatan 10 in Jakarta, again using the Pasar Turi telegraph system for the domestic exchanges were in chaos. Eri Sudewo picked up the phone in the asrama, thinking I was calling from Jatinegara, close by, making fun of him by telling him about weapons raids.

He was astonished when I finally convinced him I was in Surabaya and even more excited when I went into the details of the killing of the Dutch civilian action leader Meester Ploegman over the flag incident, and the sheer number of weapons now in Republican hands. Eri Sudewo had been intending to send us independence 'policy pamphlets' which was about as far as Jakarta had moved, but on hearing our news he thought it better to send manpower reinforcements to help me. I was proud and relieved to hear that Surabaya was clearly leading the mass actions and arms seizures, for that had been a dream of mine since working in the anti-Japanese underground.

Our youthful exuberance and dreams of freedom fortunately clouded our vision, narrowing our actions to the smaller step-by-step gains of seizing weapons as the first stage in winning control of one city in the vast Netherlands Indies. Had we taken a more mature, realistic view of the size of our task, in confronting the soldiers of Asia's strongest power, the Japanese, and then arming for a battle against the victorious British-Indian Army fresh from successes on mainland Asia, we would probably have considered it such a daunting task that it would have remained another unrealised utopian dream. That seemed to be the situation in Jakarta, where they were still talking about circulating pamphlets! We were planning an armed revolution that would either lead to our annihilation, filling the graveyards with tens of thousands of our bravest youth, or we would win the first totally free patch of territory for the new Republic and change the balance of power in the region by setting an example for other colonised peoples.

Come the challenge, came the boys, and the men to lead. By very great fortune we were soon to realise Surabaya had been blessed not only with the explosive power of a 100,000 young street fighters, obsessed with the desire for freedom, but also blessed with the emergence of mature elders whose wise, cool heads, harnessed those forces. The admixture of age and youth inspired us to believe that our street fighting capacity would somehow cope with the powerful enemy line-up against us. Then, as now, half a century later, the challenge still seems so daunting that only the unwise, or the obsessed, would have plunged into the blood pool forming around us in those last weeks of September that grew to an ominous, threatening size during October 1945.

THE FEARSOME BAMBOO RUNCING WARRIORS

We had experience that enabled our street fighters to...launch attacks with demonic intensity...they manifested a ferocity that was akin to amok, a desperation that no enemy could withstand for long in face-to-face combat because...they showed scarce concern for their own safety. The Japanese, on the other hand, had surrendered, and were a bit out of practice, having had little else to do on Java but bully defenceless people for three years. Mount Fuji would be a sight to restore their spirits, not the spectre of 10,000 raggedy, angry Surabayan kids pointing spears at them.

We were young, and blinkered. We were on a path to freedom, and we were yet to comprehend the true size of our probable losses and sacrifices. At this stage, late September 1945, a quite unanticipated phenomenon arose in Surabaya where individual youths, who had missed out on seizing weapons for themselves, began arming themselves by sharpening bamboo spears. This raised the stakes in confronting Japanese military compounds and barracks, where guards sat behind deadly machine guns. But I knew they feared the *runcing* bamboo spears, even behind a machine gun because sheer numbers would overwhelm them in these raids. When the attackers did get through they stabbed their victims repeatedly, in the stomach and eyes.

The Japanese Naval Headquarters at Gubeng, where the bamboo spear fighters were also poised to attack, was our next target. The main entrance faced the Kalimas River and its gateway opened to the road along the Kalimas banks. Gubeng viaduct and Station were close by. One side of the Japanese compound was protected by tall razor wire fencing, and a railway line that further down ran behind a Middle High School (HBS *Hooger Burger School*). The Japanese were isolated, as on an island surrounded by city streets and housing.

Our BKR unit had no special plans to go into attack that morning, so I was surprised that for once our HQ was almost empty, with just a few older men and women from the kampungs helping us with logistics. Not a recruit in sight! I then heard they were all out, with thousands of others, surrounding the huge Japanese Navy compound. This was typical of the quickening pace of revolutionary activity in Surabaya. Between the months of August and early September actions were sporadic; now in late September we attacked anything and anyone whether we were armed with spears or firearms. We were not quite a cohesive force by any means, still relying on 'mass ambush psychology,' but we were getting there.

We now had experience that enabled our street fighters to react quickly to any situation and launch attacks with a demonic intensity; they manifested a ferocity that was akin to amok, a desperation that no enemy could withstand for long in face-to-face combat because in that state they showed scarce concern for their own safety. The Japanese, on the other hand, had surrendered, and were a bit out of practice, having had little else to do on Java but bully defenceless people for three years. Mount Fuji would be a sight to restore their spirits, not the spectre of 10,000 raggedy, angry Surabayan kids pointing spears at them.

BREAK-OUT SOLDIERS KILLED TRYING TO RUN DOWN YOUTHS

On my way to the Gubeng showdown, my squad and I arrived at the crossroads of Ambengan and Ketabang streets where we saw a small armoured car disabled, with its tracks broken from an obvious attempt to ram through a cement road block. One Japanese soldier lay dead by the car, and another was on his back, dying in agony on the side of the road. One of our boys put him away with a single shot. That breakout showed signs of Japanese desperation and I surmised they had been going to get help.

Satrio "Kriting", a high school student I knew, and friend of my younger brother Suharyono, approached me as I looked at the driver, saying "I shot him, with this!" and he held up an old, long 6.5 mm Dutch military rifle. I moved off when I heard continuous machine gun and automatic rifle fire from the viaduct area near the Gubeng compound. An elderly woman had been shot through the back, by stray bullets. Satrio told us the enemy – he meant the two dead Japanese – had driven the armoured car through the razor wire fence at the crowd, before snapping its tracks and overturning on the roadblock.

My formal military training in situations like these was no help. The attackers were facing a well-armed, well-trained, disciplined force of perhaps one battalion of Japanese marines, well protected by razor wire fences, walls and ditches, in strategic defensive positions with a commanding view. I took my group, ducking and weaving through the throng of youths preparing to attack, to get within 50 metres of the perimeter fence. The street fighters seemed mostly armed with just bamboo spears, clubs, knives, swords and occasional firearms.

As we moved forward someone called to us: "Where are you heading?" We soon saw we couldn't advance further because of the men crowded ahead of us, waiting to attack. "We can't shoot for fear of killing our own." The voice belonged to a young boy sitting behind a machine gun, with two friends sitting alongside preparing to feed him extra ammunition. If he fired at the Japanese, he would also shoot the boys.

I told the machine gunner we were going up front to assess the situation, and to be careful when he opened fire. On our way forward we passed many youths who had been there for some time, impatient for a fight and now feeling the heat of the day, perhaps also hungry. They were armed with a strange variety of weapons, and now faced a defensive wall of sharpened poles and razor wire.

They lay prone and squatted or stood as they shouted insults at the Japanese as only the *Arek Surabaya* can. We could still hear shooting from the viaduct, facing the main entrance, then heard a boy shout: "We can't move forward, we might be hit by our own men shooting from on top of the viaduct bridge!" He pointed to the front of the compound, where ricochet bullets could be heard pinging off the walls.

The angry boy let fly with a couple of rounds against the compound wall, and others followed suit, firing at random and making a great din. We were afraid the others to the rear would start doing the same and my hair stood on end at the thought of being shot by our own men. I could hear someone shouting: "Don't shoot, don't shoot! You'll hit our own men!" It was directed at a very young boy preparing to fire a grenade launcher.

What a disaster! No amount of military training could help me here. The boy's *tekidanto* was a Japanese copy of Western, hand-held grenade launchers, capable of sending a grenade over a distance of 300 metres, and he was going to fire a lethal weapon for the first time!

Luck was on our side. The Japanese had not returned fire, so I continued my careful survey, moving towards the viaduct, where the situation was much the same, with hundreds of street fighters poised for an attack, but held back by the defensive walls around the compound.

Around midday, the sun was high and the day heating up, so I decided to return to our BKR base in Kaliasin. After working back through the attack lines where youths in their thousands were massed, I found myself once more on quiet city streets, where life in contrast was perfectly normal and people were going about their daily routines as though nothing had happened. The *becak* (pedicab) drivers were still carrying people along the roads, and the shops were open for business, soup was still being served.

Nearing our base, several truckloads of boys waving red and white national flags and fiercely shouting independence slogans brought me back to reality. The vehicles were now marked *Milik RI,* meaning the 'property of the Republic of Indonesia', and seemed to be driven around aimlessly, first in one direction, then returning on the same road. This was one of the first times I had seen *Milik RI,* but over the following months the words were to become a familiar daub on houses, factories, buildings and vehicles, and were even later used as a political slogan against foreign-owned businesses or nationalised estates.

Once inside the Kaliasin HQ, we heard news that our elders had met with the Japanese Naval Commander of Gubeng compound, Rear Admiral Shibata, which explained why the Japanese guards had not used their considerable firepower. Frankly, we didn't care if the Japanese were conferring or negotiating, that would not alter our plans. With the numbers we could now summon up, sooner or later we would get their guns. If they had indeed sent the now overturned armoured car crashing through our barriers in the hope of reaching outside help, it was an ill-conceived plan that had cost two soldiers' lives. To ensure success, they should have had supporting troops to follow in its tracks. We pondered also why the Japanese did not use their grenade launchers on us. We were perfect targets for them, penned up against their fence. My question was: would they remain passive?

We ate lunch and rested a while, then returned to Gubeng to check out the situation. We heard nothing of the progress of the 'high level' talks. At Gubeng, mid-afternoon, the place was eerily quiet because our boys who a few hours earlier were pounding at the fence had now gone away, perhaps to lunch! They had left a litter of bullet shells and puncture marks in the cement walls. We continued, down an embankment of the road surrounding the compound, through long grass, to Locomotive Street. Still not a person to be seen!

The boys may have withdrawn because they heard there were talks between the leaders and the Japanese, or perhaps they had simply gone home for a rest after lunch. There was no logic in the mob movements. But I wasn't happy seeing that territory emptied, an emptiness even more marked because the perimeter fence was now bent and leaning where the crowd had pushed against it. The supporting walls had remained because of the razor wire support. The silence had me reminiscing of a more carefree era, to a similar sunny afternoon in 1931 when I was a curious ten-year-old schoolboy, standing in the long grass in that very same place waiting for grasshoppers to spring.

Moving very cautiously, I took my squad through the panelling of the outer wall by breaking open a section, then going under the razor wire into a very quiet enemy compound. We were on nervous alert, warily taking in the surrounds. The path used in our schooldays no longer existed, but the ditch was still there, offering cover. In such moments of stress, the mind wanders down old pathways and I now took a moment to register dismay that the Japanese had chopped down my old, favourite Jackapple tree that we climbed to pick the fruit before scrambling up an iron trellis to get to Locomotive street level as a shortcut home.

We moved slowly to a hut where we found a small armoured car, empty, with no weapons, and behind it some buildings used for stores. Inside the first store we found stacks of good quality Japanese leather military boots, as well as spare parts for motor vehicles and heavy, filled drums. No weapons or ammunition.

I ordered the others in the squad not to remove any materials, no matter how tempting. But Mulyono, a tiny boy whose cheap rubber sandals were torn and barely holding together, whispered to me he wished to put on a pair of boots, and leave his sandals in return. "I'm exchanging, not stealing," he said, with a poker face. The humour of his claim won me over. In his entire young life he would never have owned a pair of leather shoes, let alone good boots. I told him to hurry, because it would have been an ignominious end to his young life had he been shot while putting on a pair of stolen boots. For years I enjoyed conjuring up images of the surprised Japanese soldier who on opening his locker would discover his boots had been magically transformed into two twisted bits of stinking rubber.

We continued our search with heightened awareness. I sensed the enemy was not far from us, but could not detect the direction, so we moved to a big yard where trucks were parked and almost stepped on a sprawled, stiffened body of a Japanese soldier who appeared to have been shot dead as he tried to mount a Harley Davidson motorcycle. There was a small bullet hole in his head and the blood around it had congealed. It looked like his own men had shot him, with a 6.5 mm Japanese Arisaka carbine.

We moved a few steps further to the corner of a building that blocked our view to the left. To continue walking upright we would have risked being seen on the open ground of the motor pool, so I began to crawl, and without instruction, the others followed suit. Soon, I saw something ahead of me that made my heart pound furiously, and sent me into the immediate reflex of releasing the safety on my rifle. What lay ahead was another scene that I would never forget as long as I lived: a field as big as a football ground packed with row after row of Japanese soldiers. They were sitting down, holding their rifles vertically, all with bayonets fixed, unmoving. Hundreds of bayonets shone in the bright afternoon sunlight like a thousand lights.

I retreated a little and gave a sign for the others to remain quiet while they came to see for themselves. They uttered no words, but I could hear their gasps as they quietly moved back past me, stunned by the scene. What should I do? Should I open fire and empty the entire magazine on the Japanese we considered the enemy? That would have been suicidal. The others in the squad were observing me, awaiting my decision. I was outwardly calm, but internally unsure. Were these soldiers on the alert, with fixed bayonets, awaiting a result of the talks? We withdrew quietly.

After arriving safely back at the BKR base in Kaliasin I imagined all those Japanese soldiers at the ready, like loyal and obedient troopers, when hundreds of our boys had been at their fence earlier. If ordered they would have attacked us, fighting to the last man, until our numbers would have overwhelmed them, but they would have taken hundreds of us out. On reflection, I was certain they had been ordered to simply remain alert. Had they intended to attack they would have equipped their armoured cars with machine guns. This was a good sign. We might get more Japanese weapons without open, costly warfare.

After I reported what I had seen that afternoon to Dul Arnowo, Bung Wahab and others, they were astonished that the Japanese appeared still ready to fight because they had been told the talks with Shibata at Gubeng had gone smoothly. The next day, matters did go smoothly, with the Japanese marine unit in Gubeng agreeing to move out peacefully to a marshalling point, leaving their weapons, which we would now claim as booty.

We had word that Rear Admiral Yuchiro Shibata was responsible for ensuring the move was made without bloodshed. Dul Arnowo, one of the most senior of the pre-war nationalists, admitted he was still hopeful we could win our freedom without major bloodshed, whereas the youth, including myself, were convinced the Dutch would never negotiate a peaceful settlement. They wanted to regain sole rule of the Indies and they would use the British to help them. Our leaders had not yet reached our stage of thinking, though to give them great credit, they were quickly realising that neither the Dutch nor us were in a mood to compromise.

Nonetheless, a form of compromise had taken place after all, at Admiral Shibata's residence, with Sungkono and other nationalist leaders who spoke at the Tambaksari meeting. Sungkono had convinced the Japanese that the attackers massed around the Gubeng compound had only one demand, and that was to get hold of weapons to fight the Dutch, not to kill Japanese. Shibata gave in, and agreed to hand over the weapons. He ordered a subordinate officer to take a document to the Gubeng Commander. Our police chief, Mochamad Yasin, formally co-signed the document as Commander of the Indonesian Police Unit so that it would be recognised by the Allies, who had agreed in Jakarta that an indigenous police force was needed. All that was so very politely handled, but it concealed the realities: the Japanese had no option but to get out, and avoid being hammered to death at the hands of mobs, a waste of men whose ambitions now were to return home to Japan to rebuild their lives.

4

THE FALL OF THE KEMPEITAI

After that Gubeng confrontation was finished at the end of September, the only remaining Japanese power centre was the dreaded Kempeitai, whose secret police headquarters, dungeons and armoury were in well-fortified headquarters in front of the former Provincial Government Office/Building in Pasar Baru. They showed no signs of leaving, or bartering their weapons. Where the Kempeitai were concerned, our emotions wavered between fear and new confidence. We had more than 100,000 youths we could call on, but I suspected the boys themselves would need no prompting to get at the Kempeitei compound.

KAMPUNG ORGANIZATIONS TAKE SHAPE

While still pondering the Kempeitai attack, I reviewed the positive aspects of our growing but still raggedy-looking street fighters in the kampungs who were meshing well with our more formal BKR unit. The kampung youths appeared undisciplined, but they had formed their own armed, defensive systems, with each kampung choosing their own leaders in the traditional *Sinoman* manner. The adults had feared a crime wave when they saw how many teenagers were carrying weapons but, to their astonishment, crimes within their communities were rare.

Those of us with military training, with the Japanese in PETA or the Heiho auxiliary, had a fair understanding of light infantry weapons, so we placed those with experience among the kampung groups as weapons instructors. We ordered them not to take over leadership of the groups, but to allow the kampung people to elect their own leaders. We need not have concerned ourselves for they quickly chose their own leaders and organised their units without much help from us. The adults had formed auxiliary units to run community, mobile kitchens, first aid training, and communications systems using motorcycle messengers.

WEAPONS TRAINING AMONG THE 'BRIGANDS' OF SURABAYA

Although the kampung youth were amenable to weapons training and had organised themselves well, they had a lot to learn in a short time. I saw a boy try to fire a carbine with its magazine still packed in grease and had to teach him to wash the weapon down with petrol and dry it with a rag. One of the BKR Kaliasin boys brought in a mine complete with a magnet to show how it attached itself to metal on tanks or armoured cars, scaring everyone with the carefree way he handled it. Later I heard he had been in an anti-tank operation and we never saw him again.

Hand grenades were a problem, too. Some boys blew themselves up, not understanding there were several types of grenades, with differing times elapsing between pulling the pin and detonation. Hundreds of them had been handed out casually after weapons raids, like fried bananas, to untrained boys. The Japanese grenades were different from the yellow painted grenades the Dutch military used, which we called "pineapples." The Japanese, through their propaganda films in cinemas had depicted a "hero" pulling a pin with his teeth and throwing a grenade at the enemy, so they copied it, but doing that with the British or Dutch grenades they blew themselves up. In summary, tens of thousands of kampung people were training as street fighters, armed mostly with pistols, carbines and grenades. Those with no weapons carried sharpened bamboo spears and wooden clubs.

By Saturday 29 September, the day the British troops landed, Surabaya city and perimeter villages and towns like Gresik and Mojokerto were as prepared as they could be and keen to attack whoever seemed to threaten their newly won freedom. The British, who did not recognise the Republic, had instructed the surrendered Japanese not to allow weapons to fall into our hands. Some Japanese may have sympathised with our independence aspirations but we had no choice but to raid their compounds for weapons, and deal some hard lessons to certain Japanese guards who had been particularly brutal during the occupation.

The Dutch, naturally, did not recognise the Republic, blaming the resistance on 'brigandage,' and still expected Indonesians to welcome them back. This naive approach was largely to blame for the foolhardy decisions made by successive, obstinate British officers who offended the East Javanese Republican leaders by refusing to acknowledge our right to self-rule.

Dr Hubertus J. van Mook, who had aspirations to being Governor-General of the post-war Netherlands Indies, frequently used the term 'brigandage' to describe any independence uprising. Van Mook's 1945 attitudes were distinctly less enlightened than his pre-war years when he had campaigned for an independent "Indies" nation whose citizens would be anyone born in the Netherlands East Indies. The Dutch in Holland still saw the Indies and its populace as their possessions. If we wished for self-rule, we had no option but to kill the foreign troops sent in to suppress our freedom movement. But first, we had some old scores to settle with the brutal Kempeitai.

KEMPEITAI IN OUR SIGHTS

With all the Japanese armouries and outposts ransacked the Kempeitai HQ in Pasar Baru was now the sole remaining major Japanese military post intact. Was it a coincidence we left it to last? This should have been the first of our targets, an organisation feared and hated for its brutality and cruelty. My opinion was that we had gone about it in the right way, striking first at easier, low profile targets while building our strength for the big one.

The Kempeitai headquarters were indeed considered luxurious. The massive building with ancient Greek style architecture and its tall cylindrical pillars was the pride of the Dutch architects of the era. The building had been known as the Hall of Justice (*Raad van Justitie*) and was symbolic of their discriminatory colonial rule. The matters dealt with in the Hall of Justice involved only Dutch, foreigners or natives the Dutch considered worthy of rank. A rare exception was when Bung Karno was tried in the *Raad* but otherwise matters for *inlanders,* as Indonesians were called, were dealt with in the *Landraad*, and this name gave rise to the common expression for someone brought into this lower court as having been '*landraaded*'.

The Kempeitai was widely feared by ordinary people, by workers, by officials at all levels and even by the police and PETA. This terrifying organisation had spies everywhere and dealt out harsh punishments. Our underground independence movement members had proof that when the Japanese had landed they sought out the former members of the Dutch intelligence organisation (PID) and kept them on as part of their own network of informers. We called these Indonesian plain clothes spies 'cockroaches' because their main function seemed to be to undermine their own people's independence aspirations. The PID had files on most of our pre-war nationalist leaders, so were useful to the Japanese. But we also knew that many of these cockroaches got what they deserved for their traitorous work. After milking the informers of all they knew, the Kempei shot and dumped them. Many just disappeared never to be seen again. The Kempei had liquidated them to ensure their own security, fearing that deep down the informers were still loyal to the Dutch.

The Kempeitai organisation had a long reach, and unlimited power, functioning as both judge and executioner, as well as strictly policing their own soldiers. Groups of five to twelve Kempeitai troops could often be seen patrolling the streets to ensure both Japanese troops and the general public were kept in order. They would march, faces expressionless, wearing white armbands inscribed with red kanji characters, armed with oversized pistols in specially made, closed holsters. They wore leather shoulder belts that added to their fearful presence, despite their simple and often faded uniforms. These Kempeitai packs would march in step, swinging straight arms, forcing people in the street to make way for them. This was the unconcealed element of this repressive force.

The concealed element was even more deeply feared. Everyone knew of someone who had been taken by the Kempeitai, never to be seen again. In our area it was Rachim, Abdul Azis, Sukayat, Pramuji and the popular entertainer Cak Dulrasim, who was dragged away after a show in the GNI hall for comparing Surabayans to "caged birds" under Japanese rule. We had first-hand reports that his Kempeitai torturers had pumped water into his stomach then jumped on him, one of the most painful, slow deaths possible.

Cak Dulrasim was an admirer of Dr. Sutomo and came from an ancient, respected family with a history of anti-colonialism. He spent his last days giving his *ludruk* shows in the Gedung National Indonesia where Dr. Sutomo was buried. We felt sure it was former PID agents who had reported his comments to the Japanese because he did his shows in a local dialect the Japanese would not have understood. His disappearance fuelled the people's fear and hatred of the Kempeitai.

Our nationalist leaders Cak Dul Arnowo and Ir Darmawan Mangunkusumo had also been jailed several times by the Kempeitai and suffered serious health problems after their release. Arnowo, a former journalist, had been trying to keep up nationalistic spirits among colleagues, saying the Japanese empire they found so oppressive, would not last forever. A cockroach reported the comment to the Kempei who beat him and threw him into a pitch-black dungeon for weeks. His eyesight was permanently damaged.

THE ASSAULT ON THE KEMPEITAI

At dawn around 0545 hours on the first day of October the street fighters began to stir. By 0600 hours the light of the day had flooded into the kampungs and the gentle sounds of adults from surrounding kampungs moving around quietly, as children slept on, reached us. The aroma of coffee was in the air, from our own kitchen in the HQ and from the households beyond our perimeter. The murmuring we heard was nervous, anxious commentary on today's big target, the Kempei, as we called the compound. Just mentioning the organization still gave us the shivers, despite our recent good run of weapons seizures. The Kempei had a solid fortified compound, machine guns in place and platoons of men within those walls to hold us off. No one we knew had ever been inside the compound. Even local drivers working for the Kempei had only a sketchy idea of its numbers and firepower.

Planning! I tried planning how we would go about it, but nothing really came. I couldn't deceive myself into thinking I had much influence during mass attacks, but I liked to try. Once great numbers of us began to move towards a target we were like a human wave that spilled over into the streets as water will do in floods, taking all before it. I would not have much influence in the "shape" of the attack, which squad to lead, where to send scouts, which team to use to set up artillery in the rear, and so on. I was also just a deputy commander. There were many more senior to me, such as Wahab.

As the light grew stronger around 0700, I saw smoke curl up from the kampungs and heard the clanking utensils and soft chatter as the boys drank more coffee and ate cold *martabak* omelette, saved from the night before. Some would have prayed by now, perhaps promising to do the Mahgreb late evening prayer, but none in between, expecting to be busy with the Japanese. The kampung *kabar angin,* rumours, news, gossip and excited chatter all focused on plans to hit the Kempei today. Not just any Japanese target, as our previous morning sessions had decided, when everyday was a scramble for weapons. Now we wanted to hit the most dangerous of our targets.

Our success so far had been remarkable. In the final week of September youths with a mix of Surabayan Peoples Security units, had broken into and seized the contents of every armoury, ammunition or military material storehouse in Greater Surabaya. Ruslan Abdulgani, who wrote the first history of the Battle for Surabaya, later estimated that 300,000 of us were armed in some way by 30 September. Light machine guns (LMGs), pistols, rifles, bayonets, thousands of hand grenades, scores of grenade launchers and mortars and even some heavy artillery operated by former Heiho and PETA soldiers trained on these difficult weapons, were now in our hands. We placed the cannons along the beach to the north of the city in Gresik, Kedung Cowek and Kenjeran. The biggest haul from Japanese ammunition dumps came from Batuporon over on Madura Island, half of which we had shipped into rural East Java as reserve, should we fail to hold Surabaya. It was an instinctive strategy, one devised by intelligent, forward thinkers.

MONDAY-TUESDAY 1 OCTOBER 1945:
THE END OF THE KEMPEITAI

With a mixture of fear and hatred in my heart, I joined a massive gathering of fighters comprising BKR Security units and general fighters in the long-awaited attack on the Kempeitai HQ. I was armed with a Colt 32 and an Arisaka automatic rifle with cartridge belt, and took up a position facing the rear of the Kempeitai compound. The Flora cinema was behind me, across the road. My position was not far from Jalan Bubutan, in the Kawatan and Maspati district of town, a place I knew well because I had been born there on 12 May 1921, not far from where I now stood. A strange coincidence that gave rise to the fear that I might also die there, a fear I had to dampen.

The Kempeitai was the true test of strength for our fighters and our belief in self-rule as a Republic. Surabaya was the only city on Java to disarm the Japanese, by mass ambushes or by forcing the commanders to surrender weapons and step away to avoid bloodshed. But while the Kempeitai remained we were vulnerable because the British would soon arrive and use the Kempeitai to buttress their own troops to crush us.

As we moved towards the target, I went through the deliberate actions of loading and checking the ammunition in my weapons, to relieve the feelings of tension. Some shots had already been fired in the Pasar Baru area near the Governor's office. Kempei windows well ahead of us opened, but no firing came from them. Suddenly behind me came more firing. It was the main surge of youths, hundreds of them flowing toward the Kempeitai. Other, smaller mobs were emerging from the Maspati and Pasar Turi area to join the main bunch, shouting as they advanced. They carried a mixture of firearms and clubs and many had bamboo spears. They moved in a jumbled formation and all seemed in aggressive, high spirits, which they enhanced by continuous slogan shouting: "*Maju! Maju! Maju!* Advance! Advance! Advance!"

THE END OF KEMPEITAI POWER IN EAST JAVA

Any formal effort to organise these boys into a more disciplined advance or to coordinate their firing would have failed. My military knowledge was useless here because *all tactical principles had merged into one: Advance!* Despite that I still wanted to try a tactical manoeuvre, so I fired off a few quick rounds at the open windows in the Kempeitai building and shouted to my BKR unit to do the same. That gave some cover to the advancing masses because behind those windows surely the enemy waited. The masses pressed on, shouting *Advance! Advance!*

After reloading I joined the front group and was carried along by the waves of frenetic youths. On reaching the perimeter of the Kempeitai building, some began to run into the rear entrance, under a hail of fire from the open windows. I was still moving forward, or more accurately, I was pushed along, to the right of the building with a number of others ahead of me. The fighters were now under the windows, but unable to get into the building because the ledges were too high.

Away to the north we had artillery, but our men often couldn't fire for fear of hitting their own men. Similarly those in the rear with mortars and grenade launchers could not use them for fear of inflicting casualties on the men up ahead. The calls of *Advance! Advance!* were still ringing out, although the advance had come to a dead end with many of the fighters now cornered in the yard, unable to move. They had intended to use the artillery and the grenades to blow the Japanese apart if they didn't surrender, but that was now impossible.

At the moment I could only flatten down, taking cover to avoid the Japanese fire from the windows and the shells flying overhead from the boys on the viaduct. Added to those dangers was the firing from the rear by young boys using rifles they had seized just a couple of days earlier and were still learning to handle! I let a couple of pointless shots off at the open windows to keep the Kempeitai troops back inside. I wouldn't hit anything, but the action of shooting gave me confidence. The Japanese troops inside the building were now unable to keep firepower pressure on us, being hampered by their own anti-aircraft protective nets covering the building. Bunkers that ran almost the length of the front of the building also hampered our advance. Abdul Wahab had joined me at the front line and had even tried sneaking up on the Japanese from the side of the building but was shot through the thigh, and carted off to hospital. They had snipers at the high windows.

THE STREET FIGHTERS 'STACKING' AGAINST KEMPEITAI WALLS

The daring leaders of the attack made it to the base of the steps leading up to the wide veranda but there were held back by Japanese fire, taking a few casualties on the way. Many took cover where they could, but the few who kept going were quickly shot dead and their blood splatter stained the grey marble floor.

That setback sent the boys crazy. They ran amok. Those under the windows flat against the wall were screaming and poking their bamboo spears and clubs into the wall in frustration. I was hemmed in and felt my whole body shaking and flushed. I still had both rifle and pistol fully loaded but I couldn't use them. A boy alongside me had taken a grenade from his belt and made as if to throw it, but I stopped him because he would have been unable to get a good swing and it would have dropped short and killed us all. His eyes were flaming red and he was speaking unintelligibly, perhaps swearing at me, but he finally understood and held on to the grenade.

Most of the others around me were still firing at the open windows and the main building to keep the snipers inside. Wounded men were being carried or dragged out of the action to a safer place at the rear, through the crush. The stink of sweat and gunpowder stung the nostrils. I wondered what the Kempei had planned, then remembered the Japanese had not used grenades on us in our attack on the Naval Base at Gubeng a few days earlier, or used grenade launchers, which would have slowed down the waves of attackers. During my military training with them, the Japanese emphasised bayonet combat and we were thus intensively trained. When one finally came face to face with the enemy, it was then a matter of life and death, and the better skilled survived. I was sure they would now come at us with bayonets and in our crowded front line we would be easy targets. I looked around at the main throng and saw, with some alarm, that there were no leaders among them, just a mass with a single desire to overrun and kill the enemy. I took the lead, fixed my bayonet with a shaking hand, looked left and right and saw others following my lead. Perhaps it was me who next shouted the order, "Fix bayonets!"

About that time, the shooting on our side slowed, then stopped. Then came a call for ceasefire, passed on from man to man, starting from the front of the building. In the following lull that fell over the combat area, fire brigade sirens could be heard in the distance. Surabaya's famous well-muscled firemen were joining in the attack.

A silence fell both inside and outside the building. Then, slowly, word filtered through that negotiations were in progress around the front of the building, so we stopped the chatter and sat quiet. We were told that the Kempeitai Japanese leaders were now prepared to talk with us. Mohammad Yasin, our Police Chief, had come through the fence to approach the Japanese. During the very careful discussion that followed, Chief Yasin convinced one of the Kempei's senior officers to hold up a red handkerchief and wave his arm, to signal a ceasefire to the Japanese troops. That worked. The Japanese stopped shooting.

So far, so good, but there remained the important matter of removing the Kempeitai troops from this strategic building and gathering their weapons and ammunition. They may not willingly surrender the arms so we could resume the surge, with added ferocity and intensity of the kind that had obviously unnerved them, whenever we liked. They surely knew they would lose even more men if they didn't agree to a ceasefire and handover.

The Japanese were quick to remove their dead to ensure the enemy could not estimate their losses, so we were unsure of how much damage we had inflicted, but it had been considerable. Our dead were plainly there to see, being carried away one by one, along with scores of seriously wounded fighters who were taken to the 'SayBayZay', our colloquial term for the former Dutch hospital *Centrale Burgerlijke Ziekenhuis* (Central Public Hospital). An hour after the ceasefire very few of our original, massive force remained. But I was not ready to leave the scene. As far as I was concerned a ceasefire did not mean mission accomplished.

POOR MEN IN RAGS FACING THE JAPANESE ENEMY

In the silence that followed the ceasefire I took a few moments to coolly observe the boys who were risking their lives. Although they were now attached to various nationalist groups, or in the BKR Peoples Security units, they were just kampung boys who had become gallant street fighters because they wished, above all, for their freedom.

What I saw in them moved me deeply. Almost all of them were from crowded kampungs, having had little schooling. By their early teenage years they would be cigarette sellers, helping in the big marketplaces, shop assistants, or dealing in second-hand goods. As they grew a little older and stronger, they became becak drivers or took jobs on the docks or factories, or learned to be motor vehicle or sugar mill mechanics in the busy, industrial city that Surabaya had been under the Dutch. Many were unemployed, a common feature of the Japanese years, and all of them wore tattered or patched clothing that reflected the scarcity of cloth and the poverty of living under the Japanese, who had confiscated shop and factory stores. Most of the boys were shoeless, or wore cheap rubber sandals we called stinkies, that came quickly apart even with normal wear and emitted a foul odour.

In contrast to their rags, they were well armed, and their weapons shone. They had carbines, machine guns, pistols, swords, clubs, sharpened bamboo spears, hand grenades and knives. Some wore ammunition belts, had side arms in holsters and belts with clips for bayonets. They showed a steely determination, and were quickly enraged in battle. They were not fighting for a foreign ideology or a religion or any political party; their sole aim was independence, independence for our people, and for themselves, for they truly believed they could only be free if Indonesia was free. *Merdeka* for the nation and *merdeka* for themselves and their family were indivisible.

They had gathered naturally in small groups, just as I had with my BKR team, but their commitment to each other appeared somewhat stronger, perhaps because they had grown up together in the similar kampungs and been neighbours since they were small children. Their young lives for the past years had been completely dominated and determined by a cruel Japanese military government. They had been denied rights, in any form, and suffered the consequences of Japanese military oppression more than most. They had been beaten and kicked for trivial matters like failing to show respect or not dismounting from a bicycle when passing a sentry.

My status as a university student had made my life far easier. I had been given certain rights and freedom, lodging in an asrama, a fellowship and almost sufficient food. When we discussed rebellion against the Japanese we were heavy on theory and optimism, and the notions expressed in those Prapatan 10 meetings included an element of egocentricity. We had rarely suffered the way these boys had.

As I watched, they were slowly rising from their tiring prone positions to move a little more freely, standing, stretching or just resting as they sat, but always they held tight to their weapons and kept their eyes on the Kempeitai building, wary of the enemy. I knew they were hungry and thirsty, as I was. But food could wait.

TIME TO PAY BACK THE JAPANESE FOR THEIR CRUELTY

My thoughts were on revenge. Payback time. Killing the enemy who had murdered friends and family and scores of others who had disappeared, having been taken away at night, never to return. Like the tens of thousands of fit young men taken as *romusha* slaves for the Japanese army in Thailand and Burma, or worked to death making landing strips or docks for them, working under armed guards who shot them where they fell. Revenge for hundreds of our young women, held captive in dormitories in fenced compounds to be used by platoons of soldiers for sexual recreation.

The top of the elegant old Justice building was now bathed in golden sunshine as the sun was westering. By around four o'clock we were hungry and thirsty and tense. The wounds, cuts and bruises now began to throb whereas earlier we had hardly noticed them. Yet I felt I couldn't just leave the scene because someone had to be responsible for the Kaliasin BKR unit. The task of leading the Kaliasin boys fell to me entirely. We had earlier agreed that Abdul Wahab would lead the attack and I would be the rearguard. But he was in the SayBayZay, so I was now in command.

I consolidated our positions on the spot, out of the line of fire. I could hardly take my squad and leave the scene so I weighed up the situation. It was late afternoon and just 15 of us remained at the front line.

HASANUDDIN: MY FUTURE COMMANDER IN POLISI MILITER

Someone I held in high regard shared my view that it was too early to withdraw from the Kempeitai site. Hasanuddin Pasopati had suddenly arrived, and seemed pleased to see me. We had been together the evening before when he returned to our HQ with gossip that he knew of past secret negotiations with the Japanese, who, as certain defeat approached in the Pacific War, had apparently not honoured an agreement to surrender thousands of weapons to the nationalist cause in August and September. The truth was that they had very willingly followed the British Command's orders to use force to put down independence uprisings and keep weapons from us. In Surabaya we had to wrest the weapons from them and overrun their compounds to win the weapons. Now, in the face of our successful mass attacks, they were again prepared to negotiate to save themselves bloodshed.

Hasanuddin named Admiral Maeda, Rear Admiral Shibata and Major General Iwabe, who were also named in later research, as three people who were helping Atmaji, Katamhadi and Suwondo, our nationalist negotiators.

Hasan' and I had known each other in BKR circles. He knew that I had been at the Faculty of Medicine in Jakarta and had undergone Japanese military training, and also that I was a Surabaya boy. He had been a schoolteacher, trained in the Dutch Teachers Training Academy (*Kweekschool*) who then joined the Japanese-sponsored PETA and rose to the rank of Cudan Co, the Japanese equivalent of Company Commander.

He was a short, clean-shaven, fiery-eyed man who at thirty years of age was six years older than me. We were both four to ten years senior to most of our troops at the Kaliasin BKR, or any BKR for that matter. Listening to him speak loudly in his Madurese accent one may have mistakenly thought he was a little deaf. His aggression and determination for Indonesian self-rule was evident in all his loud conversations. I was never sure whether this loud manner was a product of his Madurese background or a reaction to the indoctrination of the Japanese during his military training.

Whatever the source, I could easily imagine how his students would have feared him. Nevertheless, I liked him and we became close friends.

After we had got to know each other better Hasanuddin told me stories of his youth, soccer playing, lifting weights for fitness, and how he could peel a coconut with his teeth. Looking at his muscles, I could believe his sporting prowess. I dared not ask why he practised peeling coconuts with his teeth!

Hasanuddin conversed with me in Dutch, possibly because he was nostalgic or because it was the only foreign language that I had mastered, but we were comfortable with that, and were careful not to parade our language skills when our less-educated members of the Kaliasin HQ were present.

WE DECIDE TO OCCUPY THE KEMPEITAI HEADQUARTERS

That eventful afternoon, towards sunset, Hasanuddin was on the marble steps of the Kempeitai headquarters, cursing in colourful Dutch as he noted most of the fighters had left: "Why have they all gone? Just a handful of us remain!" I too was starting to become nervous, for surely the Japanese were still inside the building, and we might be in their sights. As if reading my mind he said: "They're probably in the left wing of the building."

Using the Surabaya dialect, I told the 15 or so left in our squad: "We're going in. Soon it'll be dark." Hasanuddin then said to me in a derisive tone that Katamhadi and Pramuji and the other PRI leaders who were said to be negotiating with the Japanese 'would just have to agree to us occupying the Kempeitai building.' That dark humour was typical of Hasanuddin and a reflection of his mistrust of the Japanese and negotiations. We would decide who would occupy it.

Passing the bloodied steps, we entered the main hall and to our surprise found the power had not been cut, so we were able to switch the lights on in the front rooms. As we penetrated further into other darker, empty rooms, I felt an eerie sensation, a reaction perhaps to the bloodstains on the marble floor and walls.

It would have been wiser for me not to risk the possibility of meeting any remaining Japanese troops, although it seemed to us, as we got further in, that they had moved into the left wing of the building.

The main room was vast, with a high ceiling. A long, polished teak table stood in the middle, with chairs scattered all round. Bullet holes from our artillery units on the viaduct, or firing from the roof of the Governor's office, had punctured the walls.

Hasanuddin called us all together to talk. He requested two boys to remain on guard, outside, and was impressed when they said that had already been done, further proof that we moved instinctively in these tense, dangerous times. We all sensed the Japanese were still in the building, and close to us. To hold our positions in the building, we sent a volunteer back to the Kaliasin unit to buy food supplies for us in the Central Market nearby.

Drinking water inside the building was not a problem. In that era one could drink fresh water from the mountains straight from city taps. The night passed as in a dream with the situation developing quite differently from any scenarios I had imagined in Prapatan 10 asrama, debating moves against the Japanese. I keenly felt the sharp difference between the imagined scenarios and the reality of our situation now, more so when listening to Hasanuddin speak of his experience a few hours earlier.

Hasan' told me how the Kempei assault had been halted. On his initiative with Atmaji, Katamhadi and Suwondo from the underground, he had approached the Japanese senior officer Major General Iwabe. Hasanuddin said that Lord Iwabe, as Commander of the Armed Forces in East Java, had been amenable to the approach and promised to order the Kempeitai officers to cease firing on their attackers.

Hasan had asked the order to be made, in writing, in Japanese; then he and his group had carried the document to the Kempeitai commander, still unsure whether the Kempei would stand down. Mohammad Yasin, as Commander of the Special Police, accompanied Hasanuddin. We were waiting for an answer.

At the time I was concerned with the perceptions outside if the

Japanese were known to be handing over weapons to Indonesians, for in fact most of our weapons seizures were done by confronting the Japanese and overrunning their compounds. We had lost many men and countless of us were severely wounded in the Kempetai assault. That was hardly a gift from the Japanese.

It was now dark, and we had succeeded in occupying only a section of the Kempetai headquarters, and we were moving with great caution. I shared my fears with Hasanuddin, who responded in his usual loud voice using the tough local dialect: "You think I'm not nervous? Who's *not* afraid? These are Kempetai troops, not the regular soldiers. Shit, it's not like we're fighting three hundred geisha girls. You know the Japanese are just as likely to plant a booby trap bomb, and we'll all be blown up together." Outside, Atmadji, Rambe and Pramuji had readily "agreed" we should be the ones to sneak in here. "Terrific!" he said, calling them dimwits for choosing the safety of the BKR headquarters, while we were creeping around in the Kempetai HQ.

I cut him short, wanting urgently to know about this Iwabe document: "Surely there's more to this instruction from Iwabe? Was there anything further said?" Hasanuddin answered, with a level of optimism: "Yes, there was. I got a second letter from Pak Iwabe that his troops would be moved to a former internment camp in Pasar Malam Ketabang. I'm confident they'll go, because of the General's order."

I questioned him: "What if the Kempeitai troops refuse to leave?" Hasanuddin asked why I thought it possible, and he recalled the earlier mention of booby traps, indicating Japanese resistance. I said we also were capable of planting bombs. "We've got lots of explosives from our raid on the Japanese Naval Base. The Japs are not the only ones who can set off bombs, don't worry about that!"

Hasanuddin looked sharply at me, taking a while to determine whether I was poking fun at him: "You're truly a crazy student. It won't come to that. They'll obey *Lord* Iwabe!" In using Commander Iwabe's title, he revealed to me his confidence in the senior officer, and his handwritten documents. I was soon to discover his confidence was well placed. Hasan's intended use of the document, which no others knew existed, was to prove crucial to the Republic's chances of survival.

Hasanuddin had barely finished speaking when there came a loud shout from one of our young guards. The boy had demanded: "Who goes there?" and there was a quiet, formal response in Japanese. We waited anxiously, on alert. Soon after the exchange the boy came in smartly to report that one of his team was holding a Japanese soldier who had requested a meeting with his superiors, meaning us. Hasanuddin looked to me for an opinion.

A SENIOR KEMPEITAI OFFICER ARRIVES QUIETLY TO TALK

My mind was working like lightning. I knew the style of Japanese military thinking, and that they valued the elements of surprise and speed. This was not a hostile action. At most it could have been a probe to assess our strength, and I was a little annoyed that they had come to us and not us to them, despite our close proximity in the building. Clearly, Hasanuddin was thinking the same thing.

We permitted the Japanese to approach us. The young guard preceded a Japanese who was in appearance nowhere near anything I had imagined. We had expected a stern, well-muscled uniformed Kempeitai soldier, with a shaved head and a humourless expression. The man who entered was a gentleman in his fifties, dressed in neat, conservative civilian clothes. His haircut was more suited to a professional banker than a soldier, and he sported a thin, greying moustache that moved as he smiled to us. His very appearance put us at ease. If he was Kempeitai then surely he was from the upper echelons, perhaps in psychological warfare department or the propaganda division.

Despite his friendliness we were very much on our guard. He spoke Bahasa Indonesia, not perfectly, but we fully understood him. He mixed Indonesian and Japanese words in his conversation, and included some humorous pleasantries. He wanted to make it clear to us that for the Japanese the war was truly over.

For us, however, it was the start of a long struggle. He appeared surprised to see, now that he was close up, how young our fighters were, and how many youngsters were armed with a mixture of lethal weapons, commenting that they seemed to be all under 20 years of age. He could also see that as their officers, we were exceptions, but still very young, and he probably guessed from seeing Indonesian trainees in the PETA that Hasan' was about 30, and I about 24.

When he entered we had been busy cleaning our weapons. We had laid out on the teak table the several parts of our dismantled carbine and my pistol, both of which attracted the attention of our guest. He said, in Indonesian, something along the lines that what he saw was "Bagus, bagus, the first duty of a soldier is to clean and care for his weapon."

His eyes rested on my .32 Colt Automatic and commented, perhaps idly for something to say, that he had never seen such a beautiful weapon. I calmly picked it up and handed it to him. Hasanuddin, standing beside me, gave me a shocked stare that the old man fortunately could not see. The older man handled it carefully, saying it seemed new and was a delight to hold. While inspecting it closely, he said: "Yes, very beautiful. Made in America...good, good, thank you."

With a smile he handed the Colt back to me. We then spoke of Indonesian and Japanese food and other unimportant matters, all in a friendly tone. A little while later our guest rose to excuse himself and delivered his message: "The telephone is in the room behind you. You may use it later this evening. Good night."

Hasanuddin and I saw our guest out. He was smiling as he walked into the distance and into the night, returning to the left wing of the building. As soon as he was out of sight Hasanuddin turned on me angrily: "How could you give your pistol to that Nip? How can he be friendly, he's still the enemy. Dangerous! Lucky we weren't shot!"

I just smiled took and the pistol's magazine from my pocket

and handed it to him. "Don't worry. One of the basic principles of firearms is never to lay a weapon down unless it is empty, with no rounds in the chamber." I went on, didactically, as if reciting a lesson to him, saying if, on the other hand, the weapon is an automatic ensure the magazine is clear. I said the Kempeitai officer knew the pistol was not loaded.

"You really are a *dobol*-dirtbag!" replied Hasanuddin, accepting my reproof. "Dobol" was Surabayan slang for a seriously grubby type. I changed the subject, saying the mention of the telephone was important. It was a refined gesture, indicating he wanted to be seen to be still in control.

But who was he really? We had no idea who he was. He appeared to be one of those nameless and faceless officers dedicated to his nation and sufficiently brave to sacrifice himself for it. We never did learn his name.

That evening I learned a valuable lesson on leadership. I had been convinced the telephone would work, and so ordered reinforcements from the Kaliasan BKR. Fifteen fully armed young troops arrived. With the additional strength we could guard our position overnight, even though our numbers would be far below that of the enemy. I estimated we were outnumbered seven to one. Hasan took the first shift, until 0200, then I took over from 0200 to 0600, a shift that allowed me a nap before my watch.

On the second floor of the right wing of the building we found some bare wooden stretcher beds. No mattresses, but mosquito nets. Six of us wearily lay ourselves down on the beds that were at least lice-free, a change from the rampant lice we usually suffered during the Japanese occupation. Before dropping off to sleep I tried planning what I would do in the morning and the following day. I realised we were now in the first phase of what would be a very long battle. I finally, slowly, fell into a deep sleep. Not the little nap I had planned when I first lay down.

The next morning we heard from the medics that about 40 of our men had been confirmed killed during the raid on the Kempeitai, and at least another 67 seriously wounded, of whom many would die. We buried 24 of our dead, with honours, in Taman Bahagia, the Garden of Peace, where they and others to follow remain today in the heart of the city, along with remnants of the columns of the Ministry of Justice the Kempeitai used for their HQ. The Japanese admitted to losing 15 dead, who were buried in a special ceremony, and 14 wounded, but the Kempeitai were secretive to the end and those figures would have likely been lowered, to save face.

5

THE PEOPLE'S MILITARY POLICE FORCE

FOUNDING THE MILITARY POLICE FORCE

Late Tuesday 2 October 1945, the promised orders from Iwabe were set in motion, and the Kempeitai staff and troops began arranging their move from the Kempeitai compound to a holding complex at Pasar Malam in Ketabang, inner Surabaya. They couldn't leave that day because the Pasar Malam complex had not been properly prepared and because of the special cremation and burial ceremonies needed for the Kempeitai soldiers we had killed in storming the compound. They buried their own men separately from their regular soldiers, with a solemn ceremony underlining their special status in life as in death.

The next day, Wednesday 3 October, we formally took control of the Kempeitai headquarters and all materials therein, while the Kempeitai personnel were being transferred in eight trucks to their new compound, leaving all their weapons and military equipment to us. In keeping with a face-saving agreement, the move was carried out with precision and without fuss, and the general public was left unaware of the transfer. The Kempeitai must have been aware of the high risk of further losses should the general populace become aware that truckloads of their hated enemy, now unarmed, were being driven through the city. We were utterly exhausted.

The entire building fell into our hands. The other good news was that our force had a further 15 men after several former PETA and middle high school students and technical school students joined us. No less important was the welcome into our ranks of several drivers who had worked for the Japanese; they also brought their vehicles with them, so our unit fortuitously acquired several sedans and valuable trucks. These material additions enabled us to consolidate our positions and establish logistics for a reliable food supply. Among our new arrivals were also men we were thrilled had come to us: ex-PETA logistics specialists.

The atmosphere among us by now was one of familiar belonging rather than one of tight discipline, and so far everything had run smoothly, with Hasanuddin and I being acknowledged as leaders. Among the former PETA soldiers some called me *shodan co dono,* the Japanese equivalent of Lieutenant when privates addressed superiors. Perhaps they thought my demeanour was that of a Lieutenant. It pleased me, making me proud that they should have such confidence in me.

That night, before falling asleep, I imagined the atmosphere with the Japanese troops climbing onto trucks and leaving. How would they feel? Did they, deep down, hate us for winning? Had they imagined we were all passive people because we had been colonised by white people? They had occupied a society unprepared for freedom. Europeans had colonised us since the Spice Island days hundreds of years ago, many using Surabaya as a base for their trade, whereas the Japanese had spurned foreign intervention from the days of Vasco da Gama, who had founded the first sea route to Asia that brought along with it a flood of European traders.

For the Japanese in the Netherlands Indies, a safe distance from the battlefronts of Asia, defeat had not yet become a reality and surrender was difficult for them to comprehend. During their entire stay in Java, they had felt themselves triumphant, and did whatever they pleased on a lush green island where the sun always shone and the people appeared soft and obedient. Now, those emotions were fading, perhaps pushed aside by a natural longing to be with their families, back in their own villages.

Whatever the truth, we tried to give them the impression that we were not further insulting them in arranging for their departure to an internment camp, and that we had agreed not to deliberately expose them to further danger by exhibiting them in public for propaganda purposes. We considered our actions as moral imperatives, a way to return the favour to General Iwabe, who helped us at a strategic time, and appeared to favour our determination to be independent. I remembered also that at the Gigantic Public Meeting at Tambaksari there was not one Kempeitai soldier to be seen, perhaps an early reflection of the Iwabe approach.

While the trucking of Kempeitai staff and troops was taking place, we used the time to explore the entire Kempei building and make an inventory of the weapons, ammunitions and other materials left behind. We had not opened the weapon storage rooms on the night our senior Kempeitai visitor came because we feared the Japanese had set booby traps, and had impressed upon all our men not to open those locked rooms. We also set about removing the bloodstain from walls and the marble floors.

There is one impression from that day that even 60 years later I cannot wipe from my memory. Upon opening the door to a small room at the back of the building the scent of human blood enveloped me. The floor was half covered with long dried, congealed blood, telling a tale of torture and death. What dramas had unfolded here? Was the blood from prisoners shot elsewhere and dumped here? Or blood from *harakiri* suicides? If I had followed my heart then I would have closed the door on that room and left it intact, never again to be opened. It was a scent that in nightmares went with screams and ghostly cries.

The inventory revealed we now had sufficient weapons to fully arm a unit of more than 300. The Japanese had left us light machine guns, carbines, pistols and grenade launchers all cleaned and oiled and neatly arranged. The same neatness was evident with the ammunition boxes, oil canisters for the weapons and other equipment associated with firearms.

The condition of the carbines and the rifles particularly interested me. An impression of a chrysanthemum had been imprinted on the receiver holding the magazines but someone had tried to wipe them clear using a file, but some faint impressions remained. Was this a form of ritual? I wondered if there had been an official order, following the surrender, to remove the chrysanthemum?

The weapons I got from the raid on the Japanese compound of Don Bosco had the same imprints; later during the war of independence I frequently encountered the same phenomenon. The symbols were intact because these were unused, reserve guns, never distributed. After all, the Japanese had never seen combat in Java.It was clear the Kempeitai headquarters had been the repository for personal Samurai swords for military officers posted in other parts of Java, for we discovered a room full of swords indicating broad ownership. They were stacked neatly on shelves that reached almost to the ceiling. My delight in reflecting on the ancient times in Japan came to a sudden halt when I realised that some of these swords had been used to behead Doctor Ismael and his friends who were sentenced to death after being accused of leading the PETA plot in Blitar. Perhaps also they were used to behead a number of Indonesian intellectuals the Japanese had deceived into attending a gathering in Pontianak, West Borneo. My hair stood on end. I shook and felt cold and imagined I heard a ghostly voice among the weapons that had spilled so much Indonesian blood.

MY ONLY WAR BOOTY: TWO SAMURAI SWORDS

My intention had been to examine the Samurai swords, one by one, looking to souvenir the oldest, antique short sword that perhaps had been used in *harakiri*. The ones newly made, I passed over. By the time I had finished, the bell in the Government Office tower had rung three times for 0300 hours. I chose just two swords, one with gold trim for Hasanuddin, and another for me that was unfortunately lost or misplaced during the revolution.

In another room we came across coffin shaped boxes full of automatic pistols and revolvers and other firearms whose origin was clearly Western. There were also stacks of the finest and most expensive English, Belgian, French, German and Austrian hunting rifles, names famous worldwide such as *Holland & Holland, Greener, Dumoulin, Bayard, Sauer, Ferlach* and *Springer*. They had been confiscated from the important, wealthy Dutch and Western coffee, tea and rubber planters who bought them at the specialist Hunting Guns shop of Munaut dan Van der Linden. These guns originally cost around 2,000 guilders, a great deal of money compared to the monthly starting wage of 12.5 guilders paid to an Indonesian high school graduate.

RECRUITS RUSH TO JOIN OUR MILITARY POLICE FORCE

Hasanuddin and I shared an ambition to form a Military Police Force for the Republic. Admittedly, this was not the product of deep thinking. We were in the Kempeitai headquarters with the guns and clubs the Kempei had used for military policing, so the idea presented itself. In revolutionary times actions must be swift, so we acted that day, declaring the formation of the Military Police Unit, with the initials "PTKR": Peoples' Military Police Force.

We had no need to bother ourselves with recruiting. The boys lined up so eagerly to join they almost overwhelmed us. We had to refuse many of them because they were not yet 16. We had boys with weapons in our unit who were less than 16 so several of them burst into tears when we would not allow them to sign up as military police (MP). We told them we needed boys with at least a high school education, and some foreign language skills.

We did not wish to establish yet another armed force, of which there were scores in Surabaya at the time, with a People's Security Force in almost every kampung. Hasanuddin and I were having difficulty deciding the charter of the PTKR because we needed a force that would, like other revolutionary forces, combat the Dutch and the British when they arrived. That alone meant we would give first priority in recruiting to those who were willing to put their lives on the line for independence. On the other hand, we wanted to avoid the taint of the Kempeitai's brutal style of policing.

We were dreamily optimistic in imagining a brilliant future for the Republic and saw ourselves as the guardians for visiting dignitaries and protectors of our own leaders on formal occasions like conferences. On Thursday 4 October, we came back to earth, realising that to form a serious military police force we had to know a lot more about protocol. All we had so far was a corps of armed fighters, who doubled as a revolutionary force. We therefore had to be careful not to appear as a policing threat to other fighting units at a time when confidence was crucial to success.

The problem resolved itself the next day. The nationalist leaders in Jakarta announced that on Friday, 5 October 1945, the Republic of Indonesia would decree the formation of a national army, to be called the People's Security Army, or *Tentara Keamanan Rakyat* (TKR, later the TNI). The announcement was met with both joy and puzzlement in Surabaya.

Why had the former KNIL officer (*Koninklijk Nederlands-Indisch Leger*: Royal Netherlands Indies Army) Major Urip Sumoharjo been promoted as Chief of General Staff of the TRI (*Tentara Republic Indonesia*: Indonesian National Army) with the rank of Major General? We were puzzled that an officer who had sworn an oath to the enemy, the Queen and government of The Netherlands, would be appointed in Jakarta. It was a matter of expediency, it seemed, for we urgently needed officers with military experience for our armed forces. Jakarta saw as the solution a declaration of loyalty from former KNIL members, to the new Republic of Indonesia, and a disavowal of their oaths to the Dutch.

TWO YOUNG MEN FORM THE NATION'S MILITARY POLICE FORCE

With the blessing of the East Java provincial branch of the national People's Security Corps, we formed the *Polisi Tentara Keamanan*

*Rakyat (*People's Military Police Force, PTKR*)* with Hasanuddin Pasopati as Commander and myself as Deputy Commander.

We were instructed to play the expected, dutiful role as communicating agent between the Republic of Indonesia and foreign representatives. In brief, foreigners who came to Surabaya on diplomatic missions would be given the protective presence of the Military Police of Indonesia. It was an ambitious plan, considering we were almost certainly headed for armed conflict. We were, however, utopian in our approach to life in these months because the fears of quick death stuck to us like a shadow.

The Military Police would assist former prisoners of war, and for that we needed boys who could manage liaison work with Dutch, English and other foreigners. Surabaya had been a busy, international port, one of the world's best known in the first half of the twentieth century, with American, Australian, Greek, Norwegian, Swedish, British, Japanese, German ships trading, and their citizens working in trade offices, or in manufacturing. We expected Surabaya, as the biggest port in our planned independent Republic, to regain that stature.

We had put the MP force together very quickly. By Friday 5 October our staff and troops, to our pleasant surprise, were already working together smoothly. The staff had independently organised red armbands inscribed "MP" or "PTKR" in white lettering, and formed themselves into compact sub-groups handling transport, logistics and internal security. They worked in a spirit of what was later termed *gotong-royong,* or mutual cooperation. For transport we already had jeeps, sedans, trucks, and importantly, several motorcycles for fast courier work, and drums of fuel supplies in reserve. Hasanuddin then exclaimed: "All we need now is a rubber stamp!"

I laughed at that comment because in fact this was a "season of rubber stamps" with TKR units all wanting to have their own stationery for notices and the word *Republik,* hitherto unknown to most of us, was suddenly on rubber stamps made for government offices and even shops. Bung Uman and his beautiful wife, who had both joined our unit, had wide connections in Surabaya's business community and within hours had returned with two round rubber stamps for Hasanuddin. One stamp read *Military Police: East Java.* The other said *Military Police: Java.* Hasanuddin said to them: "You're crazy! Military Police for *all* Java?" Uman placidly replied: "Well, we're the first Military Police unit formed on Java. If you don't want it, don't use it. Use whichever one you want. It will save me going back."

The Jakarta decree creating a national army meant there would be ranks, from General to Private. Therefore, Hasanuddin and I would be given a military rank. Hasanuddin as PTKR Commander was appointed Lieutenant General and as Deputy Commander I became a Colonel.

Hasanuddin immediately got some insignia and put it on his sleeve, but for just one day. The next day it was gone. When I reported to him the day after the decree I noticed – without saying a word – that the sleeves of his uniform were unadorned. He saw I had noticed and cursed me, trying to laugh it off: "Rank insignia is still being discussed. There is still no decision on colours, shape and where they'll be attached. Fuck you! You didn't even wear yours. Now I'm embarrassed."

I remained quiet. He hadn't understood that for me the problem was not the shape of the insignia. It was the problem of accepting a high rank at a time when we considered ourselves equally responsible for winning our independence. That night it was my turn to go to my in-laws' house where Lily lived. She was in the late stage of pregnancy and our first child was due in two months. I told her that now that the TKR was officially established I would have to take a military rank, a matter that had occupied very few of my thoughts until now. "Do you want to be a soldier or not?", she asked. My reply was that I felt at home with the unranked masses. So many of us had already died in this fight, and I had just finished going into the kampungs of Ketintang, Kedurus, Sepanjang and Wonokromo, distributing ten carbines and a drum of hand grenades to young men and old alike who were prepared to fight without asking for a rank. Even my older neighbour Pak Darum of the Nahdatul Ulama did not ask for a rank.

But Lily was firm, saying that while she understood my aversion to ranking at this stage, I would soon have to come to terms with the fact that armies require leadership to provide guidance, order and discipline. My skills had earned me a high rank and I should accept the situation and use them to help my units to perform better in combat.

The phase of weapons raids had passed, but there were still raids on isolated Japanese posts, the action of 16 October 1945 being a good example. We led a Japanese military unit across the Madura Strait and landed on the mosquito-infested Nyamukan Island, just off the main Madura Island. We carried orders from Rear Admiral Shibata Yuichiro to the Japanese unit there to surrender their weapons to Atmaji, who represented the Republic.

Atmaji, a former political prisoner in Sukamiskin prison in West Java, where the Dutch had put Sukarno, had just a few days earlier on 12 October been instructed to form the Republic of Indonesia Navy, ALRI. He cast off from the former Dutch Marine base in Ujung, Surabaya, using a heavily armed former Dutch torpedo boat and returned with an amazing haul of 34 landing craft, 217 carbines, 22 machine guns, grenades and ammunition and 419 Japanese troops, who were to be put in a holding compound.

Our instincts and sporadic intelligence from outside told us the Dutch and English would soon make their move. The Dutch and Eurasian personnel who headed the anti-Indonesian campaigns had been released from prison camps on Java. They were directed from Jakarta by RAPWI (Recovery of Allied Prisoners of War and Internees) staff, and aided by airdrops.

CONSIDERING THE MP'S FORMAL DIPLOMATIC DUTIES

Although the PTKR was now official, our boys were not in the mood to begin Military Police duties. The atmosphere in Surabaya was revolutionary, not cautionary, as most policing demanded. Our recruits had the same heady zeal of revolutionaries and expected to continue as a fighting force alongside other units, as they had against the Japanese, and they expected combat against the British and the Dutch.

They would accept formal duties protecting important political leaders during diplomatic negotiations with foreign parties, or as guards on prisoner of war camps, duties they saw as appropriate in those revolutionary times, but along with Hasanuddin and I, expected to be fully immersed in armed warfare. The Military Policing would ultimately be a civilian role, but for now it must be secondary.

OUR UNIFORMS: SOMETHING KHAKI, SOMETHING BLUE...

We had not decided on a uniform for the PTKR but a group of recruits by chance got control of some harbourside godowns in Tanjung Perak that contained stacks of deep green uniforms, military boots and spare uniform material originally intended for pre-war Dutch Indies (KNIL) troops. The result was a parade of troops in colours ranging from khaki through light blue, dark blue to black. Each man was issued with two sets of deep green uniforms, one pair of military boots and a black Indonesian *pici* cap that nationalist leaders wore, made from the same material. Damiri and Uman made the picis for us. Nothing fitted perfectly, so the men swapped clothing and footwear around until they had a perfect fit. At the time in Surabaya there were plenty of seamstresses who could adjust uniforms cheaply, and our needs gave rise to a thriving cottage industry!

Hasanuddin and I discussed what uniforms leaders should wear, finally deciding on one similar to the former PETA soldiers. This included wearing swords and high boots, which looked very smart, and was what the Japanese officers had worn. Hasanuddin chose dark brown boots while I chose black, which I felt was more in harmony with my deep green uniform. In later years the TNI privates described our uniforms as 'vomit green.'

After outfitting ourselves in our new uniforms we looked in the large mirror we had placed in the picket post. I felt as though it were a different person in the mirror, someone else wearing a sword in its scabbard, a Mauser with a wooden butt to use as a club, and tall shiny boots. I looked like an actor dressed for role in a revolutionary play, but Hartadi said I looked like *de gelaarsde kat,* resembling the *Puss in Boots* character of the Marquis of Carabas, in Charles Perrault's 1697 French satire *Le Chat Botte.* Hasanuddin, also looking like the Marquis in his tall boots, missed Hartadi's point, for he was not well read. The majority of the kampung street fighters who comprised the core of the attacks on Japanese saw no need for a uniform, except for protective equipment. Anything Japanese was anathema to them, except for weaponry and footwear.

I soon discovered that wearing new leather boots was painful. My feet were being forced to adapt to the shape of the boots, whereas a softer boot would have adapted to my feet. Sweat-soaked socks helped a little, but it was a painful process. The boots kept me in agonising pain and gave me heart palpitations whenever I stood for a long time before the assembled troops, shouting commands and raising the sword for a formal honour salute to Hasanuddin as Commander. I concealed my discomfort, so the troops noticed nothing unusual, but Hasanuddin did. After one ceremony Hasanuddin flew into a rage because he thought I was parodying him by limping. He shouted: "Damn you! Don't laugh, I'm serious, my feet really hurt. For these boots to fit they have to be reshaped. Help me pull these bloody things off!" I responded: "You think I'm laughing at you? I was in serious pain out there giving you the honour salute!"

We had red, swollen heels for days but finally discovered a solution of oiling the boots over several days. (Two years later in 1947 I got a new pair of high leather boots, but recalled the pain inflicted by the earlier pair, so agreed when First Lieutenant Sunardi from Counter Intelligence expressed admiration for and wished to borrow them to show off to his mother and family in Madiun. He returned them after two weeks and thanked me. I replied that it was *I* who should thank him, for he was breaking in my boots. "You louse!" he shouted. "I've suffered for days! The skin is peeling off my feet, looks infected..." but the rest of his answer was drowned out by laughter.)

THE PTKR AND PRISON CAMPS

We were assigned the duty of security and protocol in the Darmo POW camp where Dutch internees were held. We appointed Damiri Ichsan, a former member of PETA and Hizbullah, as camp Commander. The Japanese had treated the Dutch internees harshly, intimidating and weakening them on near starvation rations, so in these post-war weeks the internees, especially the women and children, were thankful indeed for Red Cross aid packages parachuted in from Allied aircraft. Damiri helped by fetching parcels that landed wide and found several suspiciously heavy. Pistols, sten-guns and ammunition from Dutch and British sources had been concealed among food and medicine, intended no doubt for the ex-KNIL soldiers to use against our independence fighters in Surabaya. It was another example of Dutch airdrops backfiring, as their leaflet drops had. The arms smuggling impugned all the prisoners, in a way, and deprived the women of desperately needed care items for their children.

HOW WE ORGANIZED OUR STRIKE FORCE

We kept the PTKR organisation as simple as possible. Hasanuddin and I were Commander and Deputy Commander, assisted by four officers each with individual responsibilities. The main force would be used for armed assaults, secret intelligence work, and liaison, protocol and guard duties. The second group handled logistics, supplies, transport and courier work.

We intended to go into combat with 400 fully armed troopers, comprising ten Platoons of 39 plus leaders, but soon had 500 men, as volunteers arrived. Within each Platoon we had three Squads of 13 men, knowing from recent fighting that smaller groups were more effective. We were weak on communications, having no radio systems. We were in turbulent, violent and discordant times, so we prepared for the unexpected, yet we were all focused on winning our independence. The anti-Republican elements, especially released internees, accused us of bringing Surabaya into a state of "anarchism on a large scale," but they were referring to a few unstable, paranoid individuals who inflicted torture on Dutch civilians, exhibiting elements of sadism and other spiritual diseases. One of them was a Kempeitai local spy who enjoyed torturing our prisoners. We saw that as a form of over-compensation for his misdeeds as a Japanese hireling and removed him permanently. Other cowards had tortured and killed newly released Dutch POWs in the Simpang Club, holding kangaroo courts where no defence was allowed. Dul Arnowo reacted with furious anger to these criminal actions by extremists whom we sidelined where possible.

THE CHINESE 'CLOSED COMMUNITY' ACTION

One morning a group of Chinese boys arrived from Kapasan and handed over to us to investigate some Chinese they had beaten up – some with serious injuries – because they suspected them to be Kempeitai spies. They then asked for transport to finish the "clean up" in Chinatown, regarded as a somewhat closed community to native Indonesians. We gave them a big bus and reasoned that the methods they would use on other Chinese would be the best for removing the informers the Dutch and Japanese had used who were now lying low. We gave the Kapasan Chinese youths the chance to show their allegiance with our struggle for independence. They would realise that if we did the job we would be accused of racial cleansing on business people who had always been obedient to the Dutch, preferring business to politics. A swathe of Chinese were loyal followers of Sun Yat Sen's nationalist movement to free China from foreign or Communist domination and had Chinese passports. They would soon have to choose between China and our Republic, if they were to remain in Indonesia.

IWABE'S POTENT DOCUMENT

We had held on to the original Iwabe document that enabled us to move the Kempeitai Corps out of their HQ into a holding camp in Pasar Malam in Jalan Raya Ketabang. Hasanuddin and I now decided to risk a second use to remove a large Japanese strike force from a camp just out of Jombang, southeast of the city. A delegation of Jombang youths had come to us for help in disarming the Japanese. If they remained intact until the British arrived we would be in serious trouble because the British would use them to buttress their own forces against us as they had done in other cities on Java.

Jombang was one of the crucially important towns for us. Located in the Lower Brantas Valley, it was a rich sugar-growing town, one of the series of strategic towns along the Brantas Valley that included Sidoarjo, Kediri and Mojokerto that still carried elements of serious pre-war foreign plantation wealth. If we were successful we would not only be adding new weapons and materials, but also raising the profile of the PTKR by neutralising a strong Japanese force. We developed an ambitious, but dangerous plan with Hasan' and I leading a convoy that comprised three trucks carrying two teams of armed troops, and two black sedans, the types of luxury transport used by the most senior Japanese officers.

We deliberately chose not to have a big show of force in case the Japanese felt they were being cornered and had to respond with firepower. We were banking on the Japanese to follow the spirit of the Iwabe document to avoid bloodshed and praying they would not know of its original use.

The Jombang boys at the Bung Munasir headquarters were ready to join us in the attack, though we did not inform them that Hasanuddin was going to rely on a document that had been specifically drawn up to remove the Kempeitai. We stressed the need to avoid aggressive postures upon nearing the camp because the Japanese might open fire on us. We wished also to make clear to the Japanese that we had the capacity to attack, if necessary.

To achieve those aims, both the Jombang and our boys would stay back, in full view of the Japanese who would be concealed in defensive positions.

We had to advance over unknown territory, for no one in Jombang had a map of the area. Among the Jombang troops were a number of country boys armed only with bamboo spears, clubs, swords and other sharp weapons. They had no experience in serious weapons raids.

The convoy left the main road and took a narrow path just wide enough for a truck. After passing a small village where thick hedges of bamboo grew, we went into what appeared to be a broad, dry rice field that had not been worked for some time. The Japanese may have warned the locals to give them a clearing around the base for security purposes.

We ordered the convoy to stop. The troops jumped down and took their positions and the trucks dispersed. We had hoped the Japanese had heard the truck engines. The object of our mission was up ahead but we couldn't see them because they were so well camouflaged. The distance between the enemy and us was between 300 and 400 meters, the range of their small mortars. They may have thought we were bringing up field guns, or heavy mortar because we had stopped at a distance that would allow us to attack under cover of artillery fire or long-range mortar.

After ordering the troops not to let loose any fire or make any sudden movements, Hasanuddin and I, with Sumarman, got into the sedan with Sumantri, a former policeman from Madura in the driver's seat. We had deliberately chosen the black car because the Japanese senior officers used them and it would have a psychological impact. Hasanuddin, speaking in Madurese to Sumantri, told him to follow the track towards the camp. I was afraid the low-slung sedan would break down on the rough road, but after 300 meters the path flattened out and Hasanuddin ordered a halt. The three of us alighted but Sumantri the driver, perhaps not hearing the order to wait, reversed out and drove back, leaving us exposed. The three of us walked on, Sumarman leading. Our only weapon was my Samurai sword.

With my heart aflutter we paced on, Sumarman carrying a white flag attached to a walking stick. Not a single Japanese could be seen, though I felt many eyes watching us. They would have their binoculars on us so we had an advantage with the sun behind us, allowing us as far as possible to keep our expressions neutral. We were fearful of walking into a minefield, and feared we had already entered one, so with each step our nerves were truly on edge. When we got closer it was clear that the "undergrowth" we had seen earlier was in fact camouflaged drums. Their larger structures were also disguised and only a very sharp eye could detect them. Surely by now there were several machine guns trained on us from concealed positions.

Suddenly, a Japanese soldier stepped smartly out from behind the camouflage. The bayonet on his rifle glistened in the sunshine, but it was not pointed at us. He shouted, "Stop!" in Japanese, and we stopped, with Sumarman still waving the white flag. Hasanuddin said in Madurese to Sumarman: "Quick, Man, tell them we have a letter from Lord Iwabe!"

We had brought Sumarman because he understood Japanese, and he replied, shouting back in Japanese. He had to shout because we were still 40 meters away from the soldier. Whether the soldier understood Sumarman's Japanese or not we were unsure, but after a moment he turned and stepped smartly from view. As we were left standing and waiting, I began to swear quietly in the local Surabayan dialect, to relieve tension. Hasanuddin also cursed but he had much richer slang. Sumarman, a Central Javanese, relaxed, simply asked: "What's going on?" Hearing him, Hasanuddin stopped cursing, and nodded to indicate things were normal. By then I was trying hard to hold back nervous laughter, for we had both realized the ridiculous, dangerous situation we now found ourselves in. Only Sumarman, standing up waving the white flag attached to a walking stick, appeared serious. Perhaps he was worried about what further would be required of his Japanese, which we suspected was limited.

How was the enemy assessing us through their binoculars, seeing three native Indonesians in mismatched Japanese military uniforms, armed with one Japanese sword, wearing shiny, high Japanese officers' boots and wearing the nationalist piji hats tilted forward a little, showing a cloth badge of red and white? It must have been a sight to behold, the three of us stepping forward in unison, and I was not sure they would take us seriously given our youth and our mixed attire. But we had the document.

I had no further time for contemplation because the soldier we had seen moments earlier suddenly reappeared, accompanied by a senior officer. They stepped firmly toward us, a slight wind ruffling the flats of their jungle hats, making their appearance even more formidable. They stopped about five paces ahead of us and gave us a military salute. Their sharp eyes never blinked. The three of us returned the military salute. Hasan' opened the conversation by showing the letter from Iwabe and explained something in Japanese. Because the Japanese did not appear to understand what he was saying, Sumarman felt compelled to intervene and the officer, a Captain, appeared then to understand our mission. Hasanuddin ceremoniously gave the Iwabe letter to the senior officer, who read it carefully, his face betraying no emotion. When he had finished he spoke tersely, and Sumarman translated, saying the officer understood the document, adding that he required 24 hours to prepare his unit's move to Surabaya.

His words left me breathless. We could hardly believe our ears, but restrained our neutral facade. It was truly a great moment for us. Hasanuddin then made what was a most prescient and courageous move that would have important ramifications in our struggle for independence. He requested the Captain to write out a statement in Japanese saying that he had read the order and was prepared to move his Jombang detachment. The Japanese Captain complied. With a serious face, he wrote the letter that Sumarman translated into Indonesian. Deep in my heart I doubted whether Sumarman was up to understanding and reading all that the Captain had written, but I adapted to the occasion and put on an equally stern expression.

The Captain continued to explain his wishes to Sumarman and throughout this conversation Hasanuddin kept nodding his head in agreement, though I knew he barely understood the speech, for he too must have been almost dizzied by the magnitude of our success. When it appeared the talks were over, the Captain formally excused himself and returned to camp. We were relieved that the whole affair had gone smoothly without mines exploding or the sound of artillery. We turned around and were about to step away when Sumarman asked: "What about this flag? Shall I roll it up, or just throw it away?"

Hasanuddin stopped, in shock, then looked to me. I realised that what sounded like a dumb question from Sumarman was in fact a crucial one, and the wrong answer could wreck our good work. If we made a wrong move with the flag the boys waiting near the trucks, already tense and anxious, might misunderstand and launch an attack. If, for example, we were to discard the flag, or roll it up, we might be giving them the impression that the talks had failed and they would do something rash that would ruin everything. "Don't tell me I have to keep walking along waving the flag, like a lunatic!"

Hasanuddin snapped back at him: "Keep waving, fuck you! We're all in the shit if you don't. Let's head back, s-l-o-w-l-y." I remained quiet. I could hardly restrain myself from voicing my fears that something might still go wrong. When we got to the place where we had alighted we found Sumantri had backed the cars well away from the drop spot and we had to take another long, nervous walk to reach them. Hasanuddin cursed him loudly, in Madurese. The Jombang crew greeted us with loud cheers. By tomorrow night, their territory would be clear of Japanese for the first time in three years.

RECONNAISSANCE of the EAST JAVA DISTRICTS (KABUPATEN)

We had taken it upon ourselves to urgently reconnoitre the districts of East Java immediately south and west of Surabaya. Back on 12 October, Jakarta had appointed a former senior civil servant R.M.T.A. Surio, as Governor of East Java, an appointment lauded by our senior nationalists Dul Arnowo and administrator Sudirman.

The government of East Java then issued instructions to the rural centres to consolidate Republican power by flying the national red and white flag, *Sang Merah Putih,* and keeping the peace. We chose to prioritise the important Malang district, and then Lumajang, Probolinggo, Pasuruan and finally Bangil, all very important rural centres that the Japanese had ruled with an iron fist and drained of agricultural produce. Their treatment of the peasants had been abhorrent, and hundreds of enslaved *romusha* workers had been sent abroad, never to return.

We also expected that the former Dutch governor of East Java, Charles Van der Plas, who had been a powerful figure pre-war, would give the rural centres special attention if the Dutch returned to power. He would be a formidable enemy in territories that had thrived during the Dutch years, where plantations had been well run and employed vast numbers.

We had to appoint representatives in these rural areas who could report to us regularly should any anti-Republican sentiment arise. We arrived in Probolinggo late at night – sunsets were around 6.30 during October – so when we drove in at eight o'clock, we expected the town to be quiet. Hasanuddin knew several former PETA soldiers there, among them Bambang Supeno. We arrived rather regally in three of our black, Japanese officer class sedans, with drivers Ali and Bakri from our Transport division. We went directly to the home of Bung Kayat, one of our PTKR members, whose kampung yard was big enough to park all three sedans.

While we were enjoying a cup of coffee we heard shouting, growing louder as an angry mass of people armed with bamboo spears, clubs and knives had begun to gather around our cars. They were aggressive, making threatening gestures, and shouting that we were spies and enemies of the people. We feared we would be dragged out of the room and cut to pieces. Bung Kayat went out and tried to calm the mob, saying we were anti-Dutch and anti-Japanese and had come as friends from Surabaya. He spoke in what seemed a mixture of Javanese and Madurese, but his words carried little effect for it was clear the leaders of the mob had somehow determined we were Japanese collaborators. Kayat returned, reporting that the mob was out of control. We sat in high tension as the shouting continued, with me feeling responsible because the rural circuit had been my idea.

I saw Ali quietly loading his Schmeiser sub-machine gun while keeping it out of sight. He was taking a few with him, before they struck.

Hasanuddin asked our host: "What do they want?" Kayat said they thought we were spies because we had arrived in big black sedans that Japanese officers used, or Indonesian lackies working for the Japanese. They didn't believe me when I told them you were officers of the Indonesian Military Police because they saw no proof.

Hasan' cursed in Madurese: "Why didn't you tell them I was the PTKR Commander? I'm the one who issues such passes!" Bakri quickly opened the Japanese officers' briefcase he carried and shouted: "Wait! If you need blank travel permit forms, I've got plenty here, *and* the PTKR rubber stamp. All you need to do is sign."

Hasanuddin, much relieved, said: "You idiot! Why didn't you tell us earlier? Who will sign? Yes, *me!* Hurry, fill in a form listing Bakri and several others travelling with him. Don't say the Commander on the form is me."

The mob calmed down when they saw our travel permits, with rubber stamps and flourishing signatures, not knowing these were forged just a few minutes earlier. For three years they had lived in fear of their need for stamped Japanese travel permits, being slapped around when Japanese guards caught them travelling to even the next village without a permit. They admired our fancy forms, signatures and rubber stamps, pretended they understood all the writing, and then left us in peace.

Bakri's decision to carry the blank forms had truly saved us from a nasty end, but I still wanted to know why he had carried them. He said Hasanuddin had ordered him to quickly prepare for departure from Surabaya, so he just swept everything on his desk into a briefcase. "Along the way we would need petrol for the cars, to issue receipts, or order someone to report to Surabaya. These forms allow us to ride on trains without paying. There are so many requirements for us." He then added a line I recalled for years: "After all, we're in the midst of a revolution!"

I was impressed, but there was a further shock to come. His briefcase, now open for everyone to see, was a Japanese officer's case. No one commented further. We soon learned that the men accusing us of spying in Probolinggo were very much active revolutionaries and had already taken control of their town. The red and white national flags had been flying during the day we arrived, and ceremoniously lowered at night. By the looks of it, these men had dealt severely with anyone opposing the freedom movement. Without the paperwork we would not have seen another sunrise.

Bakri and Ali were special characters. Ali was of Arab descent, handsome and humorous and a good driver. He had boyish good looks that remained almost unchanged over the 16 years to 1961, when I saw him again in East Kalimantan where I was Military Commander of East Borneo Province during the confrontation with Malaysia. Bakri, also a fine friend, was later reported killed during the revolution, news that saddened me. In 1955, when I was conducting a military ceremony in Menado, North Sulawesi, Bakri suddenly emerged from a big crowd, astonishing me and the crowd by embracing me! He had no idea he had been reported dead.

With relief, we left Probolinggo that night, pleased to see that along the main roads on the return trip to Surabaya, guard posts had been set up in most towns and the Indonesian flags were flown by day, further proof that the villagers had understood the instructions from Surabaya.

NEWS OF A MASSACRE OF OUR MEN IN SEMARANG

On 15 and 16 October, we heard news from Semarang that Japanese troops under British orders had massacred hundreds of our independence fighters near the docks. We had known the

Japanese had been seconded to help the British put down uprisings in Bandung and Bogor in West Java, but this action in Semarang was rated even more serious. The massacre would probably set the Central Java freedom movement back for quite a while. The Japanese had wiped out a force of almost 2,000. News of the Semarang massacre sent our men into a rage that spurred them into a fanatical killing spree on Japanese prisoners in the Bubutan prison. Scores of youths had descended on the prison and opened fire on the imprisoned Japanese in an act of pure vengeance.

The British had now taken all major cities except Surabaya, the only city flying the Republican flag. They would be landing in Surabaya soon, and they would expect to mete out the same treatment to us. We had one advantage. The British were unaware we had beaten them to the punch and disarmed the Japanese ourselves, and had just removed their strike force from near Jombang, using the Iwabe document.

TAKING OVER THE JAVAASCHE BANK

Around mid-October our Military Police were called in to open the former *De Javaasche Bank,* renamed the *Shoming Ginko* by the Japanese. Even during the turbulent times the bank remained safe, though it was never guarded, further proof of the unusual ethics of the revolution.

The bank's existence was a hot topic of conversation among the Surabayan government leaders. Cak Dul Arnowo, Sudirman, Sungkono, Dr Mustopo and others were mindful that the Allies had just landed and were about to attack us, so they wished the bank to be opened and audited. We had no idea what was inside, but knew the vaults needed to be emptied.

We were not permitted to break into the bank building, or use explosives. Trying to find someone with the keys seemed an impossible task, until we heard from a member of the public, who had heard from a relative, who had heard, and so on, until we finally found out that the person the Japanese had entrusted to hold the bank's keys was a certain Mr Sumardi. The number of intellectuals with the Meester title among Surabayans in those years could be counted on one hand, so it was quite easy to track the man down. I sent a small team to visit Mr Sumardi, who lived in an elite residential area, asking him to come to the PTKR headquarters and bring the bank keys with him. Mr Sumardi arrived, looking pale and rather tense. He had answered the door to find a group of raggedy dressed youths holding light machine guns, some with half a dozen hand grenades clipped to their belts. That they spoke very politely to him had not appeared to soothe his nerves.

Mr Sumardi produced an ancient, fancy key and opened the bank then stood aside. Hasan' and I were present because we had no idea what banks held and wanted to witness the opening of the strong room, which was made of concrete with a steel door, and contained two big steel safes. There were stacks of useless, recently printed Japanese notes in the cash drawers, and other drawers each holding one million Rupiah. We found bulging leather briefcases stuffed with items, left for safe keeping by Japanese officers. Hasan asked what we should do. I said that at this stage we could not do much more than we were doing. If we removed the entire contents, where could we possible store them that would be safer than a bank? The safes were too heavy to move. Hasanuddin replied: "I agree. But who will be responsible for holding the keys and the combinations to the vaults?"

"They remain the responsibility of Mr Sumardi. Only now he has to report to Pak Sudirman and agree to place himself under government control." We spoke as though the very nervous Mr Sumardi was not present. "What if he cheats on us?" asked someone under his breath, but sufficiently loud for Mr Sumardi to hear. Hasan pretended not to hear. He simply said: "I agree with 'Hario."

Mr Sumardi replied, in a strained whisper, that he agreed. We closed the bank and divided the Rupiah among units needing funds. This all occurred *before* the British landed their troops.

ASSESSING OUR STRENGTHS

A quick survey gave us some good estimates of our present personnel strength, but with no confidence of accuracy, for these were confused times. We ranged in numbers from 250,000 to 300,000 men best described as young street fighters, with 50 per cent of them well armed with adequate ammunition. The former Japanese trained PETA and Heiho soldiers among them were the only ones with any military experience but none compared to the experience and skills of the seasoned British-Indian soldiers who had weeks earlier fought in Burma. We had other factors in our favour.

The youth forces by now had become reasonably well organised and trained. We had placed around city locations thousands of well-armed, street-wise fighters, organised into squads, platoons and battalions. There were heavy artillery guns, hundreds of machine guns, grenade launchers and thousands of rifles and hand grenades. An embryonic East Java Provincial Government structure had replaced the Japanese military administration, and our most famous, senior pre-war independence heroes were in place as Governor, Resident, Mayor and a Commander of our Armed Forces, into which our Kaliasin unit fitted. Just below the leaders were other People's Defence Corps leaders, and divisions of Transport and Logistics.

We had occupied at least 20 important city buildings for use as bases and offices for the leaders. We had a functioning radio station with mobile and outdoor broadcasting capabilities.

The British were in for a shock! The Dutch had apparently convinced the British that what little opposition they may face in Surabaya was a tiny proportion of a very large population. They said a few "brigands" were demanding a Republic, a small number among millions of loyal, happy subjects awaiting the return of the Dutch and their Queen!

6

THREE-DAY WAR

BRITISH WARSHIPS DOCK AT UJUNG HARBOUR

In the afternoon of Wednesday 24 October 1945 our PTKR harbour units reported that British warships were approaching the Ujung Harbour in Surabaya. We had been expecting their arrival, and on Saturday 20 October, had coordinated a final citywide search for weapons using the People's Security Forces, the general public and anyone who could help. High school teachers and students, civil servants, becak boys, labourers, mothers, daughters and sisters all joined the search for hoarded weapons, or any that the Japanese may have hidden from us in storage sheds after the surrender.

There had already been one botched attempt by Dutch officers based at the Oranje Hotel to disarm the Japanese in Surabaya, but the kampung boys had got wind of it and taken the arms for themselves. The British would arrive in greater force and not be so careless. The terms of surrender demanded that the most senior Japanese officers take directions from the British.

British intelligence of our strength seemed to be extremely poor, for they took very few precautions in the first days after their arrival, not realizing how thoroughly we had disarmed the Japanese and how widespread was the drive for independence after the 17 August Proclamation. The Japanese would have told them the size of our mass attacks, but they had dealt with uprisings in West and Central Java and may have been confident they could handle us. We had strong support in rural centres as we had proven in our recent drive through in Probolinggo, Malang, Jombang and other towns, and they would soon learn we had disarmed the Kempeitai and other armouries, and the Jombang detachment.

We were not to know the details then, but the British and the Dutch had signed a post-war agreement specifying that the reoccupation of the Netherlands East Indies would be a two-stage operation. In the first stage, Mountbatten's South East Asia Command based in Kandy, Ceylon, would have full, or plenary powers to end fighting in the islands, and during this period the Netherlands Indies Civil Administration (NICA) would be completely subordinate. In the second stage, administrative powers would be handed over to the Dutch. Dr. Hubertus J. van Mook had travelled from Australia to Kandy to brief Earl Mountbatten. Van Mook, who was the designated Lieutenant Governor-General of the Netherlands East Indies, was now in Jakarta, though he insisted on calling it Batavia. Propaganda aired on radio convinced us that Van Mook had told Mountbatten the Javanese would welcome the Dutch back with open arms. His myopic view of the post-war world was to prove costly to British ranks and the British treasury.

Details of the British arrival slowly emerged. They had brought the 49th British-Indian Infantry Brigade commanded by Brigadier Mallaby, an officer with no recent experience of active command, but ably supported by his second in command, a Colonel Pugh, who was an experienced soldier.

The Surabayan people unreservedly regarded the British in the harbor at Ujung as enemies. We would particularly oppose them bringing in Dutch officers clandestinely smuggled into their ranks. We would not oppose their humanitarian mission where the prisoners of war and repatriation of Japanese was concerned.

Because the report of the British arrival was hazy, we decided to see for ourselves. I also saw it as imperative, from a psychological standpoint, that I lead the mission. Our combat patrol arrived at the docks area, which seemed quiet, encountering only a small number of armed fighters but exhibiting fiery spirits. They had commandeered several anti-aircraft guns and heavy artillery from the Japanese. We spoke to a Naval Base PAL unit led by Mohammad Affandi, who said no British personnel had yet landed.

I visited one inexperienced artillery unit, cautiously suggesting to them their artillery was exposed, being placed too close to the edge of the pier. They were young and confident, so argued the point with me saying that from their present position they could sight their guns directly at the British ships. I didn't push my point, because they were quite truculent, but I knew they had not thought of the obvious, reverse position. If they could see the British, the British could clearly see them. A few days later I was not surprised to hear that when the action had begun on the wharves, the British began by blowing the artillery clean off the pier. I followed up the artillery positioning with Affandi, who was later to become a close friend. But the artillery boys had held to their skewed thinking, and although they had an early win, soon paid dearly.

That night nothing happened. On return we thought our time was better spent preparing for the eventual attack by digging trenches around our Military Police headquarters in Kaliasin. From there, we could use our fire to close off the viaduct, the road in front of the Governor's office and the road leading to the Turi railway station. I also knew that our building would be vulnerable to a concerted infantry or air attack because there were no other points of strength in the surrounding buildings.

Hasan and I pondered this weakness. Our headquarters appeared as an "island" at a major road intersection that led to the biggest central market, Pasar Besar, so we had to work on getting a second, alternative location, finally deciding on one in the Peneleh kampung area, an older, historic area of Surabaya on the east bank of the Kali Mas River that divided Surabaya in two. The Peneleh residents were known to be dynamic, and proud to have hosted as residents such famous nationalist leaders as Bung Karno, our first president and leading identities such as H. S. O. Cokroaminoto, his son Anwar Cokroaminoto, Sudarsono and many others. It was there that the youth movement was first launched after the First World War.

That evening I visited the Simpang Hospital to see the wounded Abdul Wahab and Satrio 'Kriting,' whose leg was broken when patrolling the Ujung docks. Wahab expected trouble and quietly asked me for extra magazines for his pistol, which he had hidden under his pillow. He said he would shoot any Dutch or English soldiers who entered the hospital. "Better to be killed fighting than surrender," Wahab said. Kriting was looking regretfully at his boot that had to be cut open to treat his foot safely. He also would not be parted from his pistol.

Everyone carried weapons of some sort! I read later that Brigadier Mallaby's Intelligence Officer, Captain Douglas, who was at the time on board the *Waveney* in the port, had surveyed the docks from the deck and said he had seen "a lot of agitated natives dashing about, armed to the teeth with bandoliers of ammo, tommy guns, rifles and grenades," a claim I could not dispute. Teenage boys in kampungs where I was giving weaponry lessons often arrived with hand grenades swinging from a belt, and carrying light machine guns without safety catches on.

ORGANISING THE KAMPUNGS TO RESIST THE BRITISH

Prior to the landing of the British in Surabaya, the Minister for Information in Jakarta's "paper government," Amir Syarifuddin, issued a diplomatically worded order to the Government of East Java telling us not to obstruct the Allies in executing their mission in Surabaya, which was:

- Protecting and transferring prisoners or war and internees.

- Disarming and repatriating the Japanese forces.

- Keeping general law and order.

At that time I was visiting the hospital and arranging other necessities, so Hasanuddin, as Commander of the PTKR East Java had attended a meeting of East Javanese government leaders and fighting units. After the meeting he relayed the Minister's instructions to the staff and me, and shared my opinion that deep down, he was unhappy with the Minister's instructions. After all, Surabaya and to a lesser extent the province of East Java, were the only truly free territories in Republican hands. Minister Syarifuddin was in Jakarta, which was under the control of British and Dutch troops, who still referred to the city as Batavia. We would have totally disregarded Amir's instructions had we known he was a secret member of the Communist Party, a fact revealed much later when he was executed for his role in an attempted Communist takeover.

The instruction was unrealistic and disappointing, for we knew the British were coming to quell the independence movement as they had in Bandung, Bogor, Cirebon and Semarang, as well as repatriate Japanese forces and make safe the prisoners of war. Their advance officers at the Hotel Oranje-Yamato had supported the Dutch officers during the flag-flying incident on 19 September.

We would follow the order, but we each intended never to let our guard down. We could feel the Surabayan people's emotive and instinctive objections to the British army's arrival. Their fears and emotions were reflected in their words and activities as they went about organizing the defense of the city. We felt it particularly in the kampungs around our headquarters, which were older residential areas for Surabayan workers. Kawatan, Maspati, Plampitan (where Ruslan Abdulgani lived) Bibis, Semut, Klimbungan, Sulung, Jagalan, Pandean, Peneleh, Genteng, Tunjungan, Praban, Blauran, Kranggan and Bubutan, all had a special history dating back to the time when the Kali Mas was a waterway for impressive sailing ships.

The occupants of these neighborhoods had suffered under Dutch colonial rule, losing their land and properties to make way for docks, godowns and other buildings tied to manufacturing and the sugar industry. That bitter experience molded the unique *Arek*

Suroboyo character in the kampung people and they nursed a deep hatred for the Dutch and their colonial oppression. In my opinion it was this characteristic mentality that powered the Surabaya revolution.

Radio speakers the Japanese had used were placed in centrally located public places where people could gather. All through the kampungs strong fortifications had been covered with camouflage netting to counter the dangers of air attack. In strategic places the nets also covered areas to be used as machine gun nests.

The fighters with Japanese weapons now regarded them as their property, a part of themselves. They would defiantly hold on to them as they would their traditional *kris* daggers, to the point where one could never attempt to take the weapons from them. To truly understand their attitudes one must have been inside the cauldron of the Surabayan revolution.

AMATEUR ROADBLOCKS NO MATCH FOR BRITISH TANKS

In the first days after the British arrival every kampung built a bunker and made space for heavy machine guns, water-cooled machine guns like the Vickers and air-cooled Japanese machine guns like the Hotchkiss. The people made road barriers against tanks and armored cars from tables, chairs and other furniture and added old automobile bodies or broken car seats and other strange items like closets and washbasins pillaged from Dutch homes.

We advised them not to place barricades in the middle of a road where they could easily be seen from a distance, and to be extremely cautious with land mines. Several kampung boys had got hold of land mines and they had a habit of digging them into asphalt and placing small flags over them signs reading *Awas Men,* not realizing the British would understand that *men* was our word for mine, as they knew *mein,* in German.

That evening lying on my hard bunk – there was no mattress – I pondered about the British. We had to know the *who* and *what* of our enemy, so I tried to recall what we had learned about them and their important role in civilization down the centuries, but

I couldn't recall much. I knew they were successful colonizers in Africa and Asia, especially India and Burma, but our knowledge of England and the British had been filtered through the Dutch education systems, so we knew about Charles Dickens, Arthur Conan Doyle, Rudyard Kipling, Daniel Defoe and other writers. The Surabayan people had experienced oppression in the Dutch and Japanese colonial systems and understood the British and the Dutch to be two sides of the same coin. For the masses, the British were *Belanda* or "English Dutch" and, whether correct or not, their attitude towards the British was hostile. That they supported the Dutch meant they were enemies of the Republic.

OUR OWN PRISONERS ISKAK, ISWAHYUDI AND SURYO

One day I had to investigate several of our own people suspected of crimes and had been handed over to us. We had holding cells at the rear of our building that may have been part of the building in the days when it functioned as the House of Justice (*Raad van Justitie*) but the Kempei may have built them when they took over this magnificent building. I took with me three disciplined boys carrying side arms and bayonet-ready rifles.

Upon entering the cell block, one of them shouted an order: "Ready! All prisoners kneel!" I was astonished because I had never given such an order myself. Every cell appeared full and I noticed a European in one cell. In the corner of each cell was a toilet and tap. That the prisoners all followed the order to kneel made me uncomfortable, but I remained calm. Then I heard my name called by someone in cell Number One. I approached and recognised Iskak, who in Dutch times was a teacher in the Dutch-Chinese Primary School at Bubutan in Surabaya. We had often gone for hunting wild boar together during school holidays. Under the Japanese rule he had become a teacher at the Ketabang Primary School. He was a talented pianist and composer. I was in awe of him because I sang one of his songs "Tanah Airku: My Country," whose lyrics and rhythm seemed to reflect our dynamic and romantic aspirations, and also because it suited my tenor voice.

Iskak knelt before me with tears streaming from his eyes. I was certain he had done no wrong, but I also had to be very careful. Any improper move on my part would cancel out any good intentions. I sent the guards away to ask the white prisoner's nationality because I didn't want them to hear what I was saying to Iskak. We began to converse in Dutch and two other prisoners approached and also began speaking in Dutch. For the third time I experienced astonishment. They were Iswahyudi and Suryo, former PETA soldiers who had been close friends since primary school. I knew both of them well. Iswahyudi had been a medical student before entering the flying school in the Dutch times, and Suryo, whose name when young was Suyanto, was a neighbor and son of Pak Suwongso, a mid-level government official in the Governor's office during Dutch times.

Deeply depressed and fearing execution, they were pleading that they had been falsely accused of crimes. I murmured to them that I would release them later that evening after the guards changed. I walked along the front of the cells and reminded the guards not to forget to give the prisoners sufficient food and water, and checked to see that water flowed from the tap and there was sufficient ventilation, all the while thinking about the tricky question of releasing the Iskak group. These were dangerous times.

I was still pondering this when I came across a prisoner who appeared to be Japanese. He crawled forward and croaked that he was not Japanese, but a PETA soldier from Banyuwangi. That could be easily verified so I had the guards bring him to my office where the other PETA boys recognised him. Certain youths had suspected him of being a Japanese deserter because he looked a little Japanese and was not carrying identity papers. The European identified himself as Australian so I sent him to the Dutch and Eurasian internment camps, a safer solution than releasing him on our streets where he would not live long if people thought he were Dutch.

That evening, Iskak, Iswahyudi and Suryo were released and taken to my office. I ordered troops who had also known Iskak as a middle school teacher to release them. Suryo requested release on his own recognisance and I had no objections. He had been arrested because he was thought to be a Dutch spy, a pitiful accusation based on a photo of him as a boy scout saluting Queen Wilhelmina during a scouting jamboree in Holland. He had been a successful scout leader and a competitor in the prestigious Surja Wirawan and Hibulwat movements. That, to me, was hardly treachery!

That evening we dressed both Iskak and Iswahyudi in PTKR uniforms and ratified them as full members. This would prevent a re-arrest should anyone resent us setting them free, although I warned them not to leave the compound for their own safety. When he was calm, Iskak related to me the unusual story of his arrest. He and Iswahyudi had been captured in his house in Tambaksari by a group of armed men whose identity was unclear. At first he suspected he was detained because he had married a Dutch girl when he was at teacher's college in Holland. Iswahyudi, coincidentally, was visiting Iskak's younger sister Suwarti. The men blindfolded them and took them to a high school building where they were roughly interrogated and accused of being Dutch spies. The leader of this rogue band was a former PETA soldier who nursed a deep resentment against Iskak, who had been promoted to a higher rank at the Tanjung Perak airfield, while he had been passed over. The false accusations were his revenge.

The three of them were held for some weeks, during which they heard shots and shouts, were blindfolded and taken outside and given mock trials and mock executions, certain they would all be shot by firing squad. Finally they were shoved roughly onto a truck and taken to our PTKR compound. Iswahyudi's brilliant career had aroused jealousy as well. He had joined the Dutch Volunteer Flying Corps (*Vriwilligers Vleigers Corps*) and went with them when the Dutch fled to Australia as a Flight Lieutenant. He was secretly brought back to Java by submarine to spy for the Allies who landed him at a quiet beach the people called Jolo Sutro.

The Japanese arrested Iswahyudi not long afterwards and I didn't ask what his fate was following that arrest – for example why he was not executed – and how he was then able to work in the Governor's office. I may have taken this further but early next morning I got a call from a unit based in the Borsumij (Borneo Sumatra Company) building near the Kalisosok prison saying they had detained Suryo and asked me his status. I had feared this possibility when I released him. I said he was the responsibility of the PTKR and I was personally coming to collect him, so I rode a motorcycle over to collect him and brought him back to the compound. He repeatedly thanked me and said he would be more careful.

He reciprocated the help I had given him by revealing to me the location of a cache of heavy weapons. His men guarded the cache. I was astonished because I thought we had stripped clean all Japanese weapons in the Gunungsari area. Suryo fulfilled his promise and the next day we collected the weapons from a godown where he had hidden them. We got 15 heavy weapons including 12.7mm machine guns. For the second time I thanked Suryo and we parted company, but I had misgivings.

Around 1500 hours that day I heard the repeated, loud blasting of a speeding car that raced into the yard with brakes squeaking. I drew my Mauser pistol and the guard ordered a machine gun leveled and ready. One of the two men who got out of the car was Usmanaji, a former PETA soldier. The other was introduced as Sabarudin, a former PETA officer, whom I had never met, but I had heard that Sabarudin had been particularly cruel to prisoners. Sabarudin shouted to me in a rough Surabayan slang, ordering me to bring Suryo to him. I wondered about this lout, so kept my pistol handy. When he saw my gun he began an appeal: "He's a traitor, a Dutchman!" There followed a heated exchange in which Usmanaji and Sabarudin used tough language and Sabarudin again claimed Suryo was a traitor and that I should not get involved. We sent him away. Suryo was safe, for the moment.

Some days later, having almost forgotten the incident by then, I heard the sickening news that Sabarudin had killed Suryo, gunning him down in the Sidoarjo public square 24 kilometers south of Surabaya.

Sabarudin escaped unpunished for his crime that time. There were several Sabarudin-types guilty of foul murder during these weeks, notably those who had taken the law into their own hands and tortured and killed Dutch civilians. Some had private agendas but most were unstable characters, burning with jealousies and hatred. Others were secret members of the Communist Party, who executed foreigners or "enemies" without cause, justifying the killings on the grounds that the Party dealt that way with all who did not follow their Stalinist dictates. They preferred anonymity in 1945, but in 1948 many joined a Communist coup attempt in Madiun.

THE START OF THE THREE-DAY WAR

On Thursday 25 October 1945 at 0800 our men saw the first of 3,000 British troops landing, under orders from Brigadier General A. W. S. Mallaby of the 49th Infantry Brigade, 23rd Indian Division, on board the frigate HMS *Waveney*, one of four warships visible to us in the waters off Ujung harbor. Later, officers Captain MacDonald and Lieutenant Gordon Smith came ashore and announced they were acting as Allied envoys to the people of East Java, and were directed to meet our Governor Surio. From the moment of the British arrival the British attitude towards our leaders and indeed our whole defensive structures was one of polite tolerance, but no recognition. The South East Asia Command recognised Dutch sovereignty.

They announced to Governor Surio their four duties: (1) Guard and evacuate women and children from the Japanese internment camp at Darmo, 10km south of the port; (2) Release Allied prisoners of war and internees held at the city jail; (3) Remove the Japanese from East Java; and (4) Establish law and order.

That same day, for the first time since holding the position, Governor Surio had called together Residents of East Java, who were the city administrators in the province for the Republic, and senior advisers including Hasanuddin, with this express prime agenda: How to defend and secure the Republic of Indonesia.

I would learn the essence of that meeting later from Hasanuddin, but those of us on lower echelons knew no details of another important meeting between the Governor and the British envoys. We were busy preparing for battle, practising rapid loading and reloading weapons and their strategic placement and moving weighty ammunition boxes, all things that might appear to be trivial matters but in the expected fighting against the British, needed to be addressed. We soon needed them.

AMATEURS PREPARING FOR A WAR AGAINST PROFESSIONALS

Having seen the Japanese army that had conquered most of mainland China and Indo-China and had easily defeated the British in Malaya and Singapore before chasing the Dutch out of our country, I knew what a professional military outfit was. We were nowhere near that level of expertise, nor had we sufficient equipment to offer genuine opposition to the professional British–Indian force that had defeated the Japanese in Asia. On the positive side, we had a mixture of home-ground advantages, and a population dedicated to the dreams of freedom, a few thousand Japanese-trained soldiers of PETA, and more than 100,000 of our street fighters who could be mobilised. They had support from adults in the kampungs who were organizing mobile combat kitchens, first aid and courier services, and ground-level intelligence gathering.

I did not share my apprehension of a quick British victory with my men, nor did our more senior leaders once express a fear of defeat. For my part, I had been lifted from a position of doubt and caution I had experienced when we first planned raids on the Japanese armories, to one of growing confidence when raid after raid had succeeded. From having just a score of fighters with adequate weapons, within weeks we had hundreds, and the numbers grew daily. Sensational acts of personal courage won for us huge hauls. Young Esa Idrus almost alone succeeded in getting scores of modern weapons from a Gunungsari depot by making the

Japanese officer in charge an offer he had to accept: Give us the weapons and we'll let you keep your life and your sword!

While waiting, we also spent time testing the strengths of helmets, discovering that from 50 meters a shot from both Japanese and Dutch carbine rifles easily holed a helmet, and that a Colt .38 bullet could penetrate a helmet at 10 meters. Helmets would be safely used for defense against bomb shrapnel, stones and clubs, or make us look very daring!

What news we were getting about talks with the British was sporadic and frustrating. We knew the British had a legitimate reason to be in the town, and only they could handle the transportation that would take the Japanese soldiers back to Japan, and the means to process and make safe tens of thousands of internees who were still flowing into Surabaya from camps in other parts of Java.

Our focus was on independence, but tempered with humanitarian concerns and the security problems the internees were creating. A big percentage of prisoners wished to go home to Holland, but a bigger percentage now spoke out opposing the new Republic and the able-bodied men among them were aggressively demanding that properties and businesses confiscated by the Japanese now be returned to them. They claimed that because the Allies had defeated the Japanese, this gave them the right to resume Dutch control.

These few days between the British arrival and the outbreak of the first bloody conflict with them were tense in the extreme. Some rash action by our lower ranks who, regarding a British attack as inevitable, might decide to fire first was a possibility. We always believed the lower ranks would bear the full force of the fight because the British were clearly going to use their proven infantry prowess for ground fighting.

We were on our own. By now the Amir Syarifuddin request for us to obey whatever the British asked was a dead letter. We were also correct, as later events proved, that our politicians in Jakarta had no comprehension of our successes. We were the only free city left on Java. The Proclamation of Independence, however noble, was in reality a proclamation of intent and if we fell, the Republic would fade and become just a passing phenomenon. Sukarno and Dr Hatta were good leaders, but if the Dutch had their way in Jakarta, they would be arrested and jailed for collaboration. We were confident we would win independence soon, but if we failed to hold off the British in Surabaya we would face many years of revolution, especially if we had lost Sukarno, the leader most likely to bind us as a nation.

The first of the British troops came into town, seemingly casual in their demeanor. Many were seen strolling through markets, drinking coffee at the roadside stalls, while others were seen settling into buildings. At 1700 hours the British officer Colonel Pugh met with Dr Mustopo, asking him to arrange a meeting of our leaders with General Mallaby the next day, Friday 26 October. In Governor Surio's office, Mallaby's officers McDonald and Smith had demanded the Governor attend Mallaby's office for the meeting, but Surio refused. Ruslan Abdulgani reported the British had then rudely walked out!

We were now convinced the British intended to turn a blind eye to the increasing number of Dutch involved in anti-Republican activities, perhaps simply wishing to do their job and get out of Surabaya. After all, the war had been over for some weeks by the time they had docked and surely their troops would be wishing to go home.

That was a faint hope. The British we encountered were confident and often arrogant. Hasanuddin had returned from the first meeting with the British envoys, swearing and shouting to us: "It is useless talking with the British. We must be prepared to die, to die, to die! We'll shoot them and the other dogs! Everyone prepare! Practice the bayonet thrust!"

Hasanuddin's temperament was to release his emotions in this way, and he got results in seeing morale lifted among the troops, who responded to his outburst that day with heated calls, "British, prepare to die! British, prepare to die!" Satisfied with the response, Hasanuddin went inside to his desk where I heard him telephoning, cursing in the local dialect. News came that the

British had just released Captain Huyer, the Dutch officer we arrested after he and a squad had parachuted in and naively attempted to accept the Japanese surrender and disarm them. Our men had taken those weapons.

Since the success of his student spies in the Hotel Oranje, Dr Mustopo had swelled with self-importance and eagerly accepted the task for himself and his staff, comprising Suyono Prawiro Bismo, Rustam Zaim and Suwondo, to represent the provincial government in talks at Prapatkurung, where he met Brigadier Mallaby. The two were unable to agree on a meeting place for further discussions after the British suggested the location be the deck of HMS *Waveney,* an offer Mustopo rejected outright, correctly judging that would compromise them.

On Friday 26 October the Governor ordered senior civil servant Masmuin, and Police Chief Yasin and T. D. Kundan, a talented Indian businessman and ardent Republican supporter, to act as spokesmen for further talks after Mustopo and Mallaby's envoys had compromised on a new meeting place in what in Dutch times had been the British Consulate building in Jalan Kayoon.

Hasanuddin came in with some backdated news: the British had acted contemptuously by secretly including in their landing group a Dutch Colonel, after they had specifically agreed not to bring Dutch officers into Surabaya. "Don't tell me the British officers didn't know that yesterday afternoon the Dutch Colonel and several officers and enlisted men landed at Ujung!" They had reportedly met in the former Dutch Officer's mess with the leaders of the Peoples Defense Corps Navy, Umarsaid, J. Selamat, Hermawan, Nizam Zakhman and their colleagues.

Umarsaid had told Hasanuddin the British had asked for the Indonesian flag to be lowered and replaced by a British flag and that the beach be cleared for 200 meters back for troop landings. They refused.

"You dope, you didn't tell me that last night," I said. He replied that he had not told me because we would both get hot under the collar and order an attack. After the BKR Navy boys had stood up to the British and refused to lower the flag, the British countered by threatening to blow the mess to pieces. It was an empty threat. The British cannon remained silent. I said I knew why their cannon were silent. Affandi's *Arek* Surabaya navy boys had their cannon so close the British could see them sighted directly on the ships closest to the pier. Placing the weapons close to the beach, which I originally thought to be a mistake, had *some* use, though short-lived.

On Friday 26 October, after the negotiations at the old British Embassy in Kayoon were over, the British launched another large-scale landing, this time establishing a bridgehead in Tanjung Perak using conventional assault tactics.

At our level, we knew very few details of the meetings between Governor Surio and the British but I was more interested in British actions than reported progress on paper. Although we all complained about the Amir Syarifuddin order from Jakarta to respect the British wishes, we had no confidence they would restrict themselves to their repatriation and humanitarian duties and I reacted with even more alarm when I knew of the second troop landing and their strategic move to establish a bridgehead. We learned later General Hawthorn in Jakarta had ordered Mallaby not to bother continuing to "parlay" with us and simply to occupy the city.

We had absolute belief in the senior leaders of the government who were conducting the negotiations, such as Governor Surio, Resident Sudirman, Independence Committee chairman Dul Arnowo and Sudirman, because they were men who kept their cool in the face of adversity. Dul Arnowo, I knew from personal experience when our young boys were giving vent to emotions after seizing weapons from the Japanese, was able to talk sense into them without puncturing their pride.

But the situation had deteriorated some since learning our leaders had agreed to Brigadier Mallaby's Friday request to occupy certain strategic buildings in the city center. They were needed, it is true, to administer their genuine repatriation and humanitarian duties. We had to admit it was a rational request, but we then discovered they had secretly included in their delegation a Dutch officer from the Dutch Submarine Service, which could have only one purpose, that of preparing the ground for a Dutch NICA administration.

During all negotiations, the British had compounded our suspicions by consistently refusing to recognise our Surabayan city or East Java administrations, and addressed our Governor in correspondence as "Mr" Surio, not Governor Surio. Given what I was learning from intelligence from the docks, sporadic reports from the strung out negotiations, and what I deduced from my own military training, I now put the PTKR on full red alert, at first light on the morning of Friday 26 October 1945. We placed artillery units out of immediate harm's way, but positioned our machine gunners in bold view, facing the main Pasar Besar (now Pahlawan) Avenue, where the British could not miss seeing them, or misconstrue our intent.

All our troops wore armbands with large red letters MP and PRKR on white background, indicating People's Army Military Police. We tensely awaited the British infantry's expected march into the city. At 0600, just after sunrise we heard the bell above the Governor's office tolling, announcing the arrival of enemy troops, unit by unit in tight formation, marching under the viaduct in broad formations that spread across the road in front of our compound. The leading troops carried the Union Jack flag, and deliberately steered the men to avoid marching on our side of the road.

That was the first close glimpse of the enemy. The flag bearers out front were clearly Europeans, although they used camouflage paint on their face. The next group was turban-wearing Indian Sikhs, many with moustaches and beards. The next were not quite as tall as the Sikhs, with different shaped eyes and complexion. These were the Gurkhas, Nepalese who were specially trained British troops, who all carried long knives similar to our *parang* blades, as well as their rifles. They marched directly to the locations agreed upon in talks with the provincial government. Then followed closely a convoy of trucks, carrying more soldiers and logistics materials. Immediately upon dismounting they began erecting defensive barricades and emergency bunkers and setting up machine gun emplacements.

Before sunset the British by subterfuge had extended their occupation points from those in the CBD area for their humanitarian duties to numerous outlying locations and commanding control of several bridges over the Kali Mas, until they had occupied the city, without firing a shot. They were quite unconcerned that they had broken their promise not to go beyond the central streets, apparently confident they were now in complete control. If Surabaya offered no resistance the British Commander in Jakarta, General Christison, could claim all major populations centers on Java to be under their control and the process of returning the Dutch NICA administration to power would soon follow.

By sunset on Friday, the Union Jack flew in all suburbs and over seven strategic city buildings:

1. The Internatio Building in Jembatan Merah
2. The Batavia Petroleum Company HQ in Jalan Societeit
3. The ANIEM electrical power company in Gemblongan
4. The Darmo Hospital
5. The Hotel Brantas in Kayoon
6. The Radio Republic Indonesia in Simpang, and
7. The Bubutan Convent

The British now treated us as a defeated people. They had reinforced their bridgehead in Tanjung Perak, Ujung, and placed troops as far into the city as the Ferwerda drawbridge. They provoked the Moluccan Youth unit by building a bunker for an armed squad right opposite them. The Moluccans, mostly Ambonese, remained calm because they were bound by the order dictated by the Amir Syarifuddin in Jakarta. The British established their CBD headquarters in the BPM petroleum only 500 meters from us, so we understood the Moluccans' discomfort.

We could not allow this situation to remain. We called an urgent meeting that Friday night to discuss ways to curb the British infiltration, agreeing the enemy had already gone too far. The kampung people were fuming because they felt the British had surrounded them by spreading their forces widely around the entire city, a typical consolidation maneuver.

We decided to take action in every kampung the British had occupied. If fighting broke out we could quickly isolate every one of their positions and disrupt their logistics supply to their outposts. For this the kampung people had effectively prepared themselves.

My reading of the situation was more positive than most. I thought Mallaby, by positioning men in only Company strength in a number of posts around the city, had weakened his overall strength. In a firefight, the British would have to avoid using artillery and mortar for fear of hitting their own troops.

On Saturday 27 October around 1100 hours, with the city now under military occupation, a British Dakota flew over Surabaya, dropping thousands of pamphlets with orders for Surabayans and East Java people to surrender all their weapons, and other Japanese materials to the Allies within 48 hours, or be shot on sight. The pamphlets featured a color photo of the Dutch Queen Wilhelmina, against a backdrop of a red, white and blue Dutch flag. Gun owners were asked to form a line to hand them in, a nonsensical request that if acted upon would see a line several miles long, an indication of how poor their intelligence was on our numbers under arms. Major-General D. C. Hawthorn, Commander Java, Madura, Bali and Lombok (Commander of the 23rd Indian Division), based in Jakarta, signed this offensive document. The aggression was now out in the open.

When confronted with this obvious deceit, Brigadier Mallaby said he was disappointed with the leaflet drop, but was bound by orders from Batavia, an excuse that did not sit well with us. Nor would it have been pleasant for the British soldiers on the ground because from that moment on matters deteriorated rapidly. Public reaction to the drop was heated and spontaneous. No more friendly coffee breaks for their troops in our market places, no more wandering unhindered through our streets!

The leaflet abrogated an agreement our leaders had struck with Brigadier Mallaby on 24 October. Mallaby continued, contrite, saying the drop had been an error. Governor Surio believed that part, but when he pressed Mallaby to rescind the order he took refuge in military protocol, saying that "orders were orders" and he had to obey both General Hawthorn and his Commanding Officer General Christison, in Jakarta, despite his own feelings on the leaflets.

For our part at the PTKR, Hasanuddin and I had no hesitation in concluding that the Dutch army would soon be arriving, whether Mallaby agreed or not, to take power. The leaflets had asked the people to be patient, saying "your government," referring to the Dutch colonial government, would soon arrive and restore peace.

My opinion was a little different from the general populace in that I thought we had been in an almost permanent state of war since their arrival. The fighting had *never* really stopped. The leaflets *were* a disaster, but for the British, not for us. The drop motivated our trained soldiers and, especially, the kampung street fighters. The leaflets were confirmation of what we had been stressing since the British docked: that the British were acting for the Dutch, and wanted to re-establish the Netherlands East Indies immediately.

That same day, the British moved from their base south towards Jalan Nyamplungan and detained the Nyamplungan BKR chairman Sutrisno, one of our Youth leaders. They had also tried to occupy the Bubutan Police building but were chased off by the Special Police led by Agen Polisi Gontha, using an armored car. The British forces retaliated by seizing any vehicles that drove past their posts. Uman's wife, who had helped us with the rubber stamps and who wore our uniform, had her car confiscated and came to me in tears saying the troops had ordered her out of her car and just driven off in it. I had Iswahyudi, the former pilot who had fed intelligence to the Allies to help them against the Japanese, write a letter of protest to the British. Perhaps because his war work was exemplary, they returned the car.

The car snatching aroused great anger among our troops and

they wanted to take immediate action, an emotional response Hasan and I understood. We could accommodate their wishes only if they removed their PTKR insignia before going into battle against the British. We were obliged to retain duality of function, fully expecting we would soon be called as neutral guardians if our Republican leaders were to again negotiate with foreign powers.

Several incident reports came in, indicating a slow-burn beginning to lead to a major clash. In Kedungdoro district several Gurkhas in a jeep began shooting off automatic Sten guns, perhaps to frighten the people. The Kedungdoro kampung boys had been among the first to confront the Japanese in Don Bosco, so they were a formidable force. Far from taking flight from the Gurkhas, they opened fire with machine gun and carbines, killing all the Gurkha troops. The Kedungdoro kampung people dragged the bodies out and almost ran amok in destroying and then burning the jeep.

The shooting put nearby kampung units on full alert and they took up positions along main roads. I was in my wife's parents' house in Kedung Klinter, which was quite close to the shooting, so upon hearing gunfire I went to investigate though it was all over by the time I got there. The kampung people had gathered the bodies of four soldiers and placed them on the side of the road and a crowd surrounded them. An elderly man in a sarung said quietly but firmly: "*Bagus*. They're dead. Bury them. Their bodies will soon stink if left there. Bury them!"

I had to return quickly to headquarters. Along the way I felt as though an ulcer had just broken. The situation was clear. The British had attacked us. We had the right to show our teeth and bite back for the honor of our people. Hasan told me that the fiery Dr Mostopo had heard about the killing and could no longer stay calm. He drove around the town approaching People's Security posts to fire up their spirits and urge them to kill the British and Dutch, and even came to our compound but couldn't meet either of us. Mustopo then went to my house, but succeeded in seeing only my mother.

My parents' house was a drop-in place for Dr Mustopo's

students, so he knew it well. The yard was big and shady with mango trees usually in fruit. My younger brother's friends gathered there with high school friends when skipping class. Later we used the yard to hide cars and motorcycles taken from the Japanese. I could imagine Mustopo's mood that night. He was tired of British deceit. They had not once abided by agreements reached in the talks where Mustopo had represented the East Java administration. We also knew our friend Mustopo was a nervous type, quick to lose his temper.

We were surprised when Colonel Pugh, a pleasantly well-spoken senior aide to Brigadier Mallaby, came to our PTKR compound to personally deliver the message contained in the leaflets. He was clearly unhappy with the foul-up over the leaflets but could only follow orders. We saw no reason to arrest him for doing his duty to attempt calming us. He returned empty handed to his headquarters in Jalan Soceitiet. By about that time Colonel Pugh would be learning that our People's Security Commander for Surabaya, Yonosewoyo had, after a meeting with Governor Surio and Resident Sudirman, decided we would answer "in a military manner" to British demands to submit and disarm. More bloodshed was unavoidable.

A BLACK DAY FOR THE BRITISH

That was an unintended signal for a concerted attack on British posts as the news spread...Several British posts were the targets...The mix of kampung people and Security Force youths then ambushed British drivers...killing all of them and dragging their bodies out and savagely dismembering some.

Commander Yonosewoyo, who had not yet set a timetable to order an attack, soon found one had been provided for him. Drivers from three PRI North, PRI Sulawesi and PRI Navy had accidentally overturned a drum barrier the British had placed as a checkpoint at Darmo Hospital and were fired upon by a Gurkha soldier. The boys returned fire, and others from the Darmo kampung, already on standby, came in to help.

That was an unintended signal for a concerted attack on British posts as the news spread all over Surabaya. Several posts were the targets of truly massive ambush attacks. The mix of kampung people and Security Force youths then ambushed British drivers in the motor vehicles, subjecting them to a fusillade of gunfire and grenades, killing all of them and dragging their bodies out and savagely dismembering some.

We ordered half of the total PTKR forces to disperse throughout the city, dividing their strength in all sectors to monitor the developments. The remaining half of the force stayed in the post functioning as combat reserves and for anticipated non-military protocol duties.

What I had long imagined had eventuated: the central command of forces was difficult to manage. At that time the main communications between posts and sections were by motorcycle courier, bicycle or walking. That made it difficult in a rapidly changing situation where kampung residents and armed groups were gathering to attack.

RRI AND REBEL RADIO PLAY IMPORTANT ROLES ON BATTLE EVE

One of our youth leaders, Sumarsono, broadcast over Radio Republic Indonesia at 1700 that evening saying that we emphatically rejected the British demands for us to disarm. Jonosewoyo and Bung Tomo followed, essentially saying the same thing, reciting slogans that included "Freedom or Death" and "Once Free, Forever Free!" (Sekali merdeka, tetap merdeka) which were variations of international slogans from the Spanish Civil War, but new to most listeners.

At 1800 hours on Saturday evening the People's Defense Corps (TKR) Command Headquarters ordered leaders of all forces, combat bodies, the first aid teams, public kitchens, transport and other groups, to be on full alert. The order went out over Radio Republic Indonesia headed by Sukirman, who at the time was helping Sutomo (Bung Tomo) get his Rebel Radio up and running. Bung Tomo's revolutionary speeches had caught the public's attention for their fire and rhythm. Many felt he was President Sukarno's doppelganger, adopting the famous man's style of speech. Although Tomo's language was coarse, his speeches struck a chord with the kampung boys, and intensely annoyed the British. They were hitting the right notes because Surabayans were not prepared to let the British destroy their hopes of *Merdeka*, convinced that every move they made pointed to a policy of reinstating the Dutch.

On Saturday 27 October the fighting continued in the night, bloody and fierce. While we were regrouping forces after the jeep killing, British troops had pounced and occupied Kalisosok prison, succeeding in freeing Dutch prisoners held by *Arek Suroboyo*. These were the Dutch officers Huyer, Roelofsen, Hulseve, Mansen, Timmers, and Van der Straat who all claimed to be members of the RAPWI prisoner of war assistance bureau.

DAY TWO OF THE THREE-DAY WAR

On Sunday 28 October 1945, the day nationalists celebrated as Hari Sumpah Pemuda (Youth Vows Day, 1928) the armed youth groups and the kampung people joined forces to ambush British positions around the city, including the posts that had since 27 October been surrounded. Bung Tomo's thunderous voice over Rebel Radio stirred the emotions of all *Arek Surabaya* as it broadcast over the "singing pole" speakers strung around the streets by staff working at Radio Republic Indonesia.

All Sunday concerted, noisy, brutal attacks on the British posts continued at Bubutan (Koblen Prison), the Kaliasin Auto Centre, the former Dutch Police HQ, Semampir, Ujung, Radio House in Simpang, the Morokrembangan airfield, the Internatio Trade Building, the Batavia Petroleum Building, ANIEM Electric Power Company, Peneleh Bridge, Darmo Hospital, Darmo Internment Camp, the Wonokromo Bridge, the symbolic land gateway to the city, our area Kaliasin, Contang, the British Consulate in Kayoon, the Ketabang Dormitory and the important HVA Amsterdam Trading Association's former palatial headquarters.

The street fighting everywhere was violent and bloody, with killings so frequent from dawn until sunset and far into the night that it seemed we were all in a hellish dream. The cries of dying and desperate men pierced the night. Our men surrounded the Radio Station in Simpang that the British had captured as a prize, and burned it down with all British soldiers inside, annihilated. Building after building the British had occupied was stormed and the troops inside hunted down and killed by youths shooting and swinging clubs wildly, each wanting to get a hit. No pity given.

After 48 hours of this mayhem the entire British occupation force, put in place by Brigadier Mallaby to crush our spirit and effectively end the independence movement, were totally destroyed. On my rounds to survey the damage, one of the younger recruits in my unit approached hoping for my attention, his face beaming with joy. He reported he had helped kill several Gurkhas who had taken up sniper positions high in densely leafed trees in the zoo, to fire on our forces. The boys had sprayed the trees with automatic fire "until they fell like ripe starfruit." He was so pleased with himself! I refrained from comment.

Hasanuddin and I knew of 20 British occupation locations ambushed, but were not able to see all of them so we restricted our presence to the various attack zones where our troops had been involved. A British company had occupied the Koblen Jail, a battle location we could easily observe because the fighting was close to our compound. The scene there reminded me of a film of an Indian attack on an old Western fort. The tall, thick-walled structure of Koblen Jail had only one main front entrance. On every corner of the prison there were guard towers, now deserted. Our men had showered the towers with bullets until they became unsafe as a vantage point for British snipers. There were no tall buildings around the prison for use as our artillery placement. We lobbed shells into the prison compound from a nearby Chinese cinema, but our shelling was ineffective, wounding only a few grazing Brahmin cattle, which made them very angry!

MOBS ATTACK AND SAVAGELY KILL FOREIGN TROOPS

The furious attackers wanted to break down the front gate, but it held fast. Finally they rammed it with an armored car and broke through into the prison, letting the angry crowd surge through. Many British and Gurkha soldiers were killed in this battle between unequal forces where the kampung and street fighters far outnumbered the British troops. Finally, the remaining enemy surrendered, 18 of them still alive. They were to be taken to our PTKR Kaliasin headquarters nearby, being shoved along. Most of them were Sikhs and Gurkhas who had shot dead many of the attackers and, now having been captured, were fearful for their lives at the hands of a mob.

The capture and transportation of the prisoners was a dangerous exercise because the kampung people were still furious at the British. We had now to take them past the densely populated kampungs of Bubutan, Kawatan and Maspati, where their desperate return fire had killed scores of youths during the storming of the prison. Hysterical mothers screamed almost continuously as they wandered among the dead, recognising sons or other family killed in the battle. Trunks and body parts lay scattered around.

A mix of kampung masses and armed units followed the prisoner procession down the road, chanting "kill, kill", even surging into the PTKR compound through the back yard. They were screaming demands for us to kill them, shouting they were Dutch NICA, and English bastards. "Kill, kill, kill, the bastards!" they chanted.

We soon lost control of the situation. Several of our PTKR troops and I went to the front of the compound in an attempt to control what had become a wild, almost indescribable situation. We were shouting for the attackers to come out of their hysteria. I drew and waved my sword to accentuate my commands, but to no avail. The mob surged upon the soldiers and massacred all 18 of our captives, butchering them, limb from limb, into a bloody pile.

Amidst this carnage a smallish man, red faced, shouting

hoarsely, came up to me demanding I give him my sword. He wore a twisted, sadistic smile and held a bent sword, dripping with blood. It was bent, perhaps because the low quality steel was insufficient to cut bone. In fury, I turned on him, recalling he had been a Japanese collaborator who had handed himself in to us. I was never comfortable with him, so we placed him in the transport section. His true character now emerged. He now sought to compensate for his traitorous work with the Japs by joining in the killing, but I fixed an accusing eye on him and he withdrew like the coward he was.

THE AMOK CONTINUES

The amok took place amidst shrieking calls, and the odor of spilled blood was pervasive, until all 18 were dead. It all happened in such a short time. Fortunately, there were no shots fired; with a rioting crowd, a single shot would have wounded or killed several. After the mob had killed, or watched their victims being killed, they slowly came to their senses. I ordered them to bury the slain British troops there and then, in our compound, and they willingly complied. The PTKR troops built a bonfire on the soldiers' graves, believing the fire would protect them over the following nights from the evil spirits of their slain enemies.

Those extraordinary events were the obvious topic of conversation for Hasanuddin and I that evening, as Commanders and Deputy Commander of the compound where the killing had taken place. He had been with Governor Surio in his residence when the worst fighting had occurred. Hasanuddin had a simplified view of the matter: "The British themselves, by occupying the city, have driven us to evil deeds. Let them feel our blades." We both doubted this was the end of the matter, agreeing we had to stay even more alert for a British reprisal.

Although I agreed, for me it was not an experience to be categorized as a military matter, for it had been the mob action that had left such vivid impressions on me. We had tried to follow military procedure in capturing and locking up enemy prisoners, but the people had become so enraged they lost control. Despite my exposure, as a medical student in Jakarta, to the spectre of death by starvation and enslavement under the Japanese, the images of the events here replayed in my mind.

The type of deadly violence that put a sadistic smile on the face of the former Kempeitai informer quickly aroused the mobs. Yet young Suratmoko, one of our PTKR recruits, had fainted while the killing unfolded around us. I would rather it not to have happened, and events of that night left me quite unable to withdraw and take a detached view. I needed a little rest so that the next day I could face all eventualities.

It was my turn to sleep at headquarters and Hasanuddin's turn to go home. Sleep came in spurts, with disturbing, sporadic rifle and automatic weapons firing in the distance. A driver in our compound was noisily tuning a truck motor, revving it continually, despite the hour. I thought, what a nuisance! Despite all that buzzing in my ears, and the recurring visions of the killings, I managed to fall into a deep sleep.

In the 72 hours following the British occupation of the city, ambushes on British positions, on British transport convoys and any soldiers foolish enough to venture out of their posts, continued without cessation. Surabaya is a city divided by the river Kali Mas, with western and eastern sectors, which restricted the British troop movements because the Kali Mas was high in flood. With their outposts located on both sides of the Kali Mas, they had to hold several of the nine bridges across the river to ensure their logistics stream, and this is where they had been trapped, as well as in buildings they had occupied.

STREET FIGHTERS BAY FOR BLOOD

The British outposts near the bridges were easily stormed and their men killed. The only outpost troops to fight tenaciously were in the guard post at the Dinoyo Bridge where they succeeded in building a strong defensive position under the bridge. But the youths poured petrol and diesel through cracks from above and set them alight.

Kampung fighters in massive numbers were easily able to overpower and destroy any trucks carrying support troops or convoys bringing food and ammunition and kill drivers and crew. They also turned en masse on Dutch civilians, women and children that the British were trying to transport to safety from internee gathering spots to safer buildings or the docks. They never made it through.

The roads were soon littered with corpses. On the first day the British had reported 38 of their men killed, with 210 others missing, presumed dead, and another 84 wounded. After the mobs had ambushed British convoy drivers from the 123rd Indian Company while taking their civilian passengers to the Docks for protection, another 170 were killed, including women and children, and 30 more soldiers reported missing, presumed dead. We knew that all but a small number of the "missing, presumed dead" really were dead. In trying to defend their posts, the British soldiers had killed at least 500 youths and kampung people and several hundred more died of their wounds. Scores were trampled in the fray, or hit by stray bullets or suffered from misadventures with explosives.

The incomplete trunks of British troops, their limbs and body parts and blobs of human flesh were scattered all over the roads. Understandably, the massacres were the only topic of conversation in that week. For the British Commander Brigadier Mallaby and his superiors in Jakarta, it was a day of agonizing reappraisal of their strategies. From my point of view it was the obvious time for the British to stop listening to the odious claims of the Dutch, who still claimed our land as their possession, and to simply finish up their humanitarian work and ship out the unwanted Japanese occupation troops. We could then get on with running our city and our province East Java, the only two areas under Republican control.

That was my utopian view but one I knew would never be realized because the British, instead of learning from their mistakes and their duplicity and abrogation of promises, would now seek revenge. I also suspected their losses were far greater than admitted, perhaps as high as 600 dead, when more bodies were fished out of the river. We heard a report later that just eight soldiers of the 123rd Indian Company had survived by semi-submerging themselves in the Kali Mas, then making their precarious way back to their base under cover of darkness.

7

DEATH OF BRIGADIER MALLABY

That morning, Monday 29 October, after the roll call parade and a formal report to our Commander Hasanuddin, who had spent the night in his home, it was my turn for a home visit. I left to visit Lily at her parents' house, driving via the Peneleh Bridge to the Plampitan kampung to drop a passenger. I had to slow down for a swarm of children on the bridge, all peering over the side into the waters of the Kali Mas. They were watching the bodies of 20 t0 30 British soldiers floating slowly down the river to the harbour, men who the day before had been ordered to hold the bridges upstream.

Only Lily was in the house when I arrived. Her mother and father were working in the community kitchens organized by neighborhood women, and consoling neighboring families whose sons had perished in the fighting. I could stay just long enough to bathe, have a coffee and look at Lily's condition as she neared giving birth. The juxtaposition of thoughts of death and birth stayed with me on my drive back.

When I reached the crossroads of Praban and Krangan in Blauran I heard the sound of low-flying aircraft. Our forces, thinking the British would begin bombing, were quick to react. Using every weapon available to them they shot at the suspiciously low flying plane with Sten-guns, carbines and even pistols, rather pointlessly, I thought. I only saw the plane for a moment but it seemed like a DC3.

The British Command in Jakarta, upon hearing the entire 49th Brigade was likely to be totally annihilated, had hurriedly pressured Sukarno to use his popularity to call for a ceasefire. We had not realized the Dakota overhead moments earlier had carried senior British officers from Jakarta bringing Sukarno and Dr Hatta to Surabaya. The British in Surabaya were in a bad spot, and needed Sukarno's help. The potshots at the Dakota, by boys assuming only an enemy would be flying over us at this juncture, fell short.

BUNG KARNO ARRIVES IN SURABAYA

Many years later the President would give his account of those days in Surabaya but until then we were to be disappointed with the ceasefire.

Our PTKR Military Police unit was given its first protocol and guard duties involving foreign representatives and our own leaders: accompany both parties to and from locations where the ceasefire was being negotiated, a ceasefire we Surabayans knew would disadvantage us. We had the British on the ropes and could comfortably have held them to the docks area while they finished their humanitarian work and shipped the Japanese back home. But they controlled what would be our Republic's capital, Jakarta, and our leaders were beholden to them.

Jakarta ordered us not to interfere with the British military Dakota after landing, an order we followed with a heavy heart. They landed unhindered and soon afterwards were able to place troops in various locations around the city. Because our East Java Provincial Government had agreed to Sukarno's appeal that we enter into ceasefire talks, the British now felt more secure. On the plane were several British senior officers – but not General Hawthorn who had ordered the leaflet drop – bringing our president and vice-president, Sukarno and Dr Hatta, and Amir

Syarifuddin who had issued the naive instruction forcing us to "welcome" the British.

The PTKR compound was in a state of high alert when I arrived, because they too had heard the plane. Bung Tomo's Rebel Radio was reporting that the President would arrive in Surabaya, at the Morokrembangan airfield. Government House had already instructed Hasanuddin to have the Military Police attend to the protocol, welcome the VIP guests, and administer the security. Sporadic shots were still being fired, but the remnants of the British occupation troops were safely back at their base on the docks.

It was our first non-combat assignment. Hasanuddin left clear instructions that I should follow. Bung Karno was to be brought directly to the house of Resident Sudirman in Van Sandick Street. This flight from Jakarta had been arranged suddenly, but we were not surprised we had not been informed earlier. Telephone and other communications systems were mostly out of order. The whole affair had been hastily arranged in Jakarta. Only later would we learn the truth of the matter, which was that the British had pleaded for help from their Command in Jakarta, saying they were cornered and could not launch an attack. The entire 49th Brigade of 6,000 men was at serious risk of total annihilation. One didn't need military expertise to draw that conclusion after seeing so many of them dead.

Only four British posts around the city remained and they were in the Hoogerburger School (HBS) building in Ambengan Street, the Darmo Hospital, the BPM Building in Soceitiet Street and the Internatio Building near the Red Bridge. And those posts were now surrounded by the armed forces of the Peoples Security Corps. Youth units and street fighters had killed almost all the troops in the other 20 or so British posts. We had now heard from the Lindeteves (*Gelinding Tipis*) building where the British were also surrounded and couldn't move. We knew this from Hasan Basri of Rebel Radio, who was listening to British radio communications between posts, thus making it five units stranded.

Late that afternoon of 29 October, the British Commander A.

W. S. Mallaby, who had ordered the disastrous occupation of Surabaya, opened talks that ended with a formal ceasefire announcement from Government House. Although this satisfied the British it did in fact make it difficult to guarantee a halt to shooting. Gunfire could still be heard, and each time a British soldier showed himself at a window in the buildings they still occupied our men would shoot at them. The British frequently returned with automatic Sten-gun fire from their strongholds without showing themselves. They would hold the weapon with one hand, raising it above the head while remaining hidden, and fire indiscriminately into the crowd. Some of our boys from a tank unit were unhappy with the ceasefire prospects so made their feelings clear by revving their tanks' engines and driving back and forth. Bung Karno sent Ruslan Abdulgani out of the meeting two or three times to stop the tanks, but after telling them to stop Ruslan would give a signal to begin again in a minute or so. Ruslan thought the ceasefire was a mistake.

Despite the tense situation the talks between the British and the East Java government leaders continued. Several agreements were achieved in negotiations with Brigadier Mallaby and his senior officers from Jakarta with our president and our Surabaya leaders and East Java Governor Surio:

- A ceasefire and a promise to uphold law and order in Surabaya.

- Parties would guarantee the safety of the people, including internees.

The demands in the leaflet dropped over Surabaya on 27 October were to be discussed the next day (30 October) between President Sukarno and Major General D. C. Hawthorn, Commander of the British forces on Java. All armed forces were to return to barracks. The wounded were to be transported to hospitals.

The Commander of the 23rd Indian Division, Major General D. C. Hawthorn, arrived in Surabaya around 9.15 on the morning of Tuesday 30 October. Two hours later more talks were started at 11.30 and continued until one o'clock in the Governor's office.

When walking to the talks, the British negotiating party would surely have seen the oil drums mixed with burning asphalt giving off black smoke that the street fighters had rolled as a protest to the Batavia Petroleum building the British used as their headquarters. The BPM was close to the Governor's office, across the road from our Military Police compound.

THE BRITISH RELUCTANTLY AGREE TO DE FACTO STATUS

A. W. S. Mallaby and Colonel L. H. O. Pugh accompanied D. C. Hawthorn. The Indonesian party consisted of Sukarno, Muhammad Hatta, Amir Syarifuddin, our Resident, Sudirman, our most senior nationalist leader, Dul Arnowo, the leader of our armed forces, Commander Sungkono, our chief of Navy, Atmaji, prominent youth activists Sumarsono and Sutomo and our Indian pro-Independence supporter, T. D. Kundan as interpreter.

The meeting ended with a de facto recognition of the Republic of Indonesia, far short of the de jure legal recognition we sought, and an agreement containing conditions and qualifications intended to avoid armed conflict. They were as follows:

1. The pamphlets signed by Major General D. C. Hawthorn dropped by plane over Surabaya on 27 October to be declared invalid.
2. The Indonesian Military Police Force to be recognized by the Allies.
3. The Allies were to limit their presence to the area of the RAPWI internment camps around HBS and the Darmo district.

Discussions between the Allies and the Peoples Defense Corps and the Republican Police Force were to be made through a Contact Bureau. The British army for the moment would share in securing the Tanjung Perak Harbor with the People's Defense Army (TKR). The British still required the area to unload medicines and food supplies. But the harbor would remain in ultimate control of the Republic of Indonesia.

The Indonesian Minister for Information, Amir Syarifuddin,

announced further details of the negotiations, requesting the People's Security Force (TKR) be recognized as an armed force, and that the Contact Bureau, to comprise several Indonesians and British officers, be formed as soon as possible.

Prisoners on each side would be returned. The administration of transporting the internees and former prisoners of war from Darmo to the harbor would continue unhindered.

After the negotiations President Sukarno and his entourage and Major General D. C. Hawthorn and his staff prepared to return to Jakarta that same day. Bung Karno had given a fine, level-headed speech over Radio Surabaya, and now he and several of his party wanted to pay a quick visit to Bung Tomo's Rebel Radio Studio in Embong Mawar 10, before leaving. I don't know whether this was a Sukarno initiative or a Bung Tomo invitation.

My duty was to handle the protocol and to ensure the safety of the President and the British representative accompanying us. I was quite uncomfortable that a British officer was in the group. He was given access to see in detail the functioning and organization of Rebel Radio, our main propaganda weapon. Rebel Radio was housed in a former Dutch house of medium size. We entered a room packed with young men and women whose intense emotions were palpable. Bung Karno spoke in an open and friendly manner, using Indonesian mixed with some Javanese and some Surabaya dialect. Sukarno was a genuine Surabayan and had always been regarded as an *Arek* by the people, especially by the Peneleh and Pandean kampung people. When he was at middle high school he boarded with H. O. S. Cokroaminoto, the founder of Sarekat Islam, the first major nationalist organization, in Cokroaminoto's home in kampung Pandean.

In the crowded studio was a fierce-looking young man, who might have been Bung Tomo's younger brother, standing by the President with his dagger at the ready to ensure no one would get close to the leader. A young girl in the crowd was sobbing uncontrollably, saying her father had not returned that day and she feared the worst. She was Tuti Antara, a well-known street fighter and journalist whose name stemmed from her profession with the Antara news bureau. Bung Tomo was agitated, heatedly asking Bung Karno why Surabayans had to stop fighting. The president smiled and replied that there already had been too much bloodshed. The diplomacy in progress should not be disturbed. The situation was now calm, but it needed to be monitored, Sukarno said. Bung Tomo continued with his fiery questions, but the noise in the room was so loud I couldn't hear him clearly. Someone near me shouted loudly: "The British shot first!"

SUKARNO IGNORES THE PEMUDA DEMANDS, ORDERS CALM

The president gave a brief speech, asking us as Surabayans to await the government's instructions, saying it was important for us to work together to advance the independence cause. He was soon leaving for Jakarta. With a twinkle in his eye, he praised the adoring youths surrounding him, and his infectious laughter won them over. The session broke up, with smiles and shouts of "Long Live! Hidup! Hidup!"

The calls, accompanied by raised fists, were the traditional calls of the Nationalist Movement called the *Pergerakan,* during the Dutch times. For those who were members of Young Indonesia, Surja Wirawan and Hisbullah, these were familiar calls. Bung Karno knew at that moment it was the right time for him to take his leave from Rebel Radio station.

I returned to the Military Police headquarters and Hasanuddin took over from me, escorting the VIP guests to Morokrembangan airfield. I had dearly wished to speak with Bung Karno, because I felt close to him. But after long consideration I decided not to try because it would appear to the British guests that I was breaching my duty to remain neutral by appearing to be fawning over the president.

But in my heart I really did want to know Bung Karno's impressions of his visit in Surabaya. Did the central government in Jakarta really understand the situation in Surabaya before he came? Why had the Jakarta Army HQ not sent troops to Surabaya as peacekeepers or military advisers? Sadly, no one was able to give a direct answer then, and we would later discover we were going to have to carry the Revolution without help from Jakarta, although as events unfolded, our struggle inspired tens of thousands of our people who lived far from Surabaya, to join us. But we had no help from the Jakarta youth groups, who failed to make headway against the Japanese, and were then outflanked by the powerful British Army in the capital.

COMMANDER MALLABY IS KILLED

After escorting the presidential entourage to the Morokrembangan airfield for Sukarno's departure to Jakarta, the Contact Bureau began its first meeting at 1500 hours. The Indonesian members in the Contact Bureau were Sudirman (Resident), Dul Arnowo (Chairman of the Independence Committee), Atmaji, Mohammad, Sungkono, Suyono Prawiro Bismo, Kusnandar, Ruslan Abdulgani and T. D. Kundan (Interpreter). The British members were A. W. S. Mallaby, Captain H. Shaw, Colonel L. H. O. Pugh, Major M. Hobson and Wing Commander Croom. In that first meeting the group appointed Ruslan, who at 30 years of age was among the youngest of our leaders, and Shaw as joint secretaries of the Bureau.

Late that Monday afternoon, when we were back in the compound we had a report that a crowd of angry agitators were still surrounding the Internatio Building and there had been more shooting, both ways. The British soldiers in the Internatio Building were shooting at the pack gathered in the street and the situation, considering we had agreed on a ceasefire, was dangerous and getting more uncontrollable as the minutes went by. I ordered a squad to monitor the situation and reinforce the troops we had there already.

I then left the compound and crossed the road to the Governor's office, to discuss the situation with Hasanuddin, who was speaking with Governor Surio, who had just returned from seeing the Contact Bureau members. When I told Hasanuddin about the developments at the Internatio building, he, as expected, released a series of curses, but concluded: "It's useless talking to the British! Wait a moment. I'll go inside and tell them in the Contact Bureau."

Hasanuddin went into the meeting room. I was waiting outside the room in what was for that era a luxurious building. We both considered the Contact Bureau meeting to be a ritual that must be endured, an unrealistic formality in complete conflict with the warring atmosphere and realities for those people outside. I waited a long time until I became quite impatient.

Suddenly the door was flung open and an Englishman hurried past. Because I thought he was approaching me I prepared to recall my English from my dictionary should he ask me a question, but it seems he was only hurrying to the toilet, desperate to unload his lunch.

Finally, Hasanuddin emerged. He informed me the Contact Bureau members would together go to the Internatio Building to stop the shooting. He ordered me to send one of our squads to the building, to await the arrival of the Contact Bureau and ensure their safety. I said that I had already sent a squad in and they had informed me by courier they were patrolling between the location of the shooting and our compound. He seemed satisfied and said: "Jamput! Pinter kon dik! You clever bastard!"

Around 1700 hours the Contact Bureau group left the Governor's office with an eight-car convoy. Hasanuddin went quickly to our compound to get a car and driver to join them. From the look on his face he was not terribly keen on the way the Contact Bureau was dealing with the shooting match between the British and the street fighters. He was also not that pleased the Bureau members were going to the Internatio Building amidst the crossfire.

In a display of diplomatic cordiality and to impress the warring parties at the Internatio Building, Brigadier Mallaby and our Dr Mursito each rode on a front mudguard with a hand on the bonnet of the big black sedan we had supplied to lead the convoy. (These days the car is usually pictured in our history books as a burnt out shell.) Upon their arrival at the Internatio, Hasanuddin was to send the car back to the compound. "Too bad if it comes back with bullet holes," he said. That was to be some understatement!

Hasanuddin was to take up his position with our squad in place, protecting the Contact Bureau. I stayed at my post to coordinate the assignment. At 17.45 a courier reported that increased gunfire had broken out around the Internatio Building and the situation was deteriorating. Hasanuddin and our squad would need more ammunition, for emergencies.

After the Contact Bureau members had arrived at the Internatio, some had tried to order a ceasefire, but were unsuccessful. Because the British troops inside the building continued to shoot, the street activists outside shot back at the soldiers inside, who never showed themselves. They crouched under the windows and fired randomly from high windows by lifting their guns above their heads. They wounded many in the crowd below, whereas the return fire from the street was futile because the British were concealed.

The situation was escalating. Someone in the crowd suggested they burn the building. They sent for petrol and oil from the locomotive yard in Sidotopo and the station at Semut. Their warning shouts to the British to leave their weapons and accept an escort to the base were ignored.

The courier reporting this to me was agitated, though standing stiffly, his shirt dripping wet and holding his carbine, at the ready. I ordered him to stand down and rest a while and have a drink while the ammunition section prepared more supplies. We were the only post close to the Internatio, so ammunition duties fell to us. The courier was Sujak, an intelligent boy who had been with us at the height of the Kempetai events and who had stayed on guard with us over night.

When reporting the move to burn the building to get the British out I suggested dynamite would be better, not the usual suggestion from a Military policeman! I sent a motorcycle courier to the PRI youth headquarters in Simpang requesting them to prepare enough dynamite, complete with detonators, to blow out the facade of the building, but dropped the idea when I heard the explosives were unavailable.

Day turned to night. The picket guard appeared, escorting a courier from Hasanuddin. After saluting he hastily reported: The shooting has stopped for a moment because leaders from the Contact Bureau are speaking to the British inside. Hundreds of our fighters are still demanding the British leave the building without their weapons. They are also suspicious of the Contact Bureau. I interpreted this as a Hasan comment that talk at this stage was not going to help. I asked him how was Pak Hasanuddin, our Commander. The courier answered: "He's still abusive!" The courier continued: "Pak Hasanuddin doesn't want any more discussions with the British in the (Internatio) building."

I asked what discussions he was referring to. One of the senior Contact Bureau members, an Englishman, and a 'Bombay man' had gone in to talk; and there had been an explosion in the sedan outside and people had run for cover. I asked where the other Contact Bureau members were.

The courier said: "When I left to come here they were heading in the direction of the Red Bridge close by. Pak Hasanuddin instructed me to tell you not to send any more troops. He has enough."

From afar I could hear hand grenade explosions and automatic rifle fire. The famished courier hurriedly ate a Japanese "ransum" army biscuit and had a drink. I ordered him to return to Hasanuddin. Just then several trucks carrying armed youths from other units sped by, shouting and singing, going to some other disputed territory perhaps. I felt like a witness to some slowly unfolding, mysterious drama.

Then I heard more shooting in the distance, which kept up until almost 22.30 hours. I looked for a red glow, the sign the Internatio Building was burning, but saw none. Not long afterward Hasanuddin boisterously returned, with two of our squads. Several them were wet though. In his usual abusive manner, he ordered them to wash and change their uniforms.

He said to them: "Stupid! You didn't have to jump into the

river!" One in the squad answered roughly: "The Contact Bureau gentlemen all ran and jumped into the river. Well, we just followed."

Hasanuddin laughed. I interrupted, wishing to know the fate of the Contact Bureau members, and why they would be jumping into the Kali Mas. I called Hasanuddin into my office, who cursed and took a seat, drinking a glass of cold coffee. Then in a serious tone he began relating what had happened.

The emissaries sent into the Internatio building were Captain Shaw and Muhammed Mangundoprojo, accompanied by T. D. Kundan, the interpreter. Hasanuddin said the Contact Bureau faced an impossible task trying to reason with the mobs of street fighters. They were out of control. Many of them had been there since early afternoon and their numbers had since grown. Hasanuddin told a colorful side story of how a boy was howling with rage after his backside was peppered with shotgun bullets.

BRIGADIER-GENERAL MALLABY'S DEATH

Hasanuddin called the picket, wanting more hot coffee and whatever food he could find. I wasn't satisfied because I'd not yet heard what happened to the Contact Bureau members. I hid my impatience and waited until Hasanuddin had begun sipping his hot coffee before asking: "Cak Hasan, what happened to the Contact Bureau members?"

He answered: "Oh, don't fret. They saved themselves. They're all home in their own homes. The Englishman is dead."

I had no idea whom he was referring to. Hasanuddin added that Dul Arnowo had gone home safely, and that Governor Surio had already been informed all other Contact Bureau members were safely home. Ruslan Abdulgani had fled the scene and jumped into the Kali Mas. Hasanuddin then astonished me by casually adding: "The Englishman killed was General Mallaby."

I asked who had killed Brigadier Mallaby, but he responded impatiently: "Enough! It's not important. The thing is the British general is dead."

I had heard the grenade explosion that had killed him, and later saw the convoy vehicles had been burned. I was worried about Muhammed, our colleague who had gone into the Internatio Building in an official capacity, but later learned he was unharmed.

It was still unclear to me which side had ordered the fighting stopped. After the explosion the Contact Bureau members had run for their lives, diving into the canal, for cover so they couldn't have given the ceasefire order. Had the British run out of ammunition and were unable to return fire? That was a possibility.

I had no comprehension then that Brigadier Mallaby's death would become such an international incident, and we would be accused of barbaric methods in our fight to win independence. That night all our units were withdrawn to rest, and to prepare for emergencies we expected to arise in the coming days. We sent men to the Jonosewoyo compound, to Sungkono and the PRI compound to gather intelligence. That night unfolded more peacefully after midnight and we were finally able to sleep in comfort under our mosquito nets, none of us realizing this would be our last deep sleep for some weeks.

AFTERMATH OF VICTORY IN THE THREE-DAY WAR

By the morning of Tuesday 30 October, we had confirmation of the death of Brigadier General A. W. S. Mallaby, and our leaders felt the ire of the British through official channels. To have a general killed was a sensation. Formal discussions on the burial were to be handled by the Contact Bureau.

Fortunately, we were not involved with his death. We learned the British had released Mohammad from the building, but still faced the question of trying to remove the troops from the buildings and transfer them to the harbor zone as part of the ceasefire agreement. This was more important to us than the Mallaby killing because it would affect the entire security situation, so we took it seriously, especially after the announcement from Jakarta by General Christison.

Lieutenant-General Sir Philip Christison, Commander of the Allied Forces for the Netherlands Indies (AFNEI) in Jakarta) had issued an ultimatum to Surabayans, threatening that "unless the Indonesians who have committed these acts" (of killing Mallaby) surrender to my forces, I intend to bring the whole weight of my sea, land and air forces and all the weapons of modern war against them until they are crushed."

This announcement further convinced us the British were ill-intentioned. Overseas news sources reported that Christison had sent for Sukarno and held him responsible for the killing of Brigadier Mallaby "by extremists, while we were in negotiations."

We answered that damaging propaganda the best we could. Dul Arnowo as chairman of the KNI East Java reported what he knew about events at the Internatio by telegram and radio to President Sukarno. In his radio speech he reiterated that the true enemy was the Dutch NICA, which opposed independence. "We can work with the Allies" he said "but not our enemy." Cak Dul's last radio speech that morning ended with a strong appeal: "Once again, I order all fighting with the Allies to be stopped. Please follow my orders. Merdeka!"

His speech was intended for overseas listeners. We knew his private view was that the British were preparing for the Dutch Civil Administration to return. Cak Dul was an experienced nationalist and he certainly understood the methods of the British and their colonial record in dealing with the peoples of the Middle East, India and Southeast Asia.

On Wednesday 31 October, after the Christison announcement, the British and Indonesian parties came to an agreement that all British forces would return to their original landing base at Tanjung Perak harbour. The Contact Bureau would continue to function and for the moment Lieutenant Pugh would take over Mallaby's role. The British troops in the Internatio Building were to be safely trucked to the Tanjung Perak area by the People's Defense Corps.

That evening a tense silence fell on the city. In a ceremony at the Taman Bahagia, we buried the last of 81 men killed in the attack on the Kempeitai, so our boys, and most of the other armed youth units were back in their various compounds, and the kampung street fighters and general populace were home, tidying up, paying respects to those killed, or just resting.

Hasanuddin must have been feeling the pressure, after Mallaby's death. He had an idea, an idea that only someone who was constantly wishing harm to an enemy could think of. He ordered me to ride pillion on a Harley Davidson motorcycle we always had on standby and head for the open road to the northern kampung areas of Kalisosok, shouting loudly as he went, "Hey, you Areks...the British are beaten...we've won! A British General blown away...Ayo! Ayo! Be prepared!" He was using a mixture of Javanese, Madurese and Indonesian. He shouted back to me: "Tonight we're just wild Arek Suroboyo, not Military Policemen. Don't stay silent. Join me in shouting!"

He was letting off steam. After several days on formal duties as MOPs, and keeping a stiff formal official appearance, he wanted to momentarily rid us of the ceremonial handcuffs. I felt like a street fighter, a revolutionary, part of the people's rebellion, not a soldier. We had only been soldiers for 25 days. We were given a riotous reception by the kampung youths, and for a brief time others followed us in trucks, shouting freedom slogans. This was more effective propaganda than pasting up flyers or writing slogans on walls as we had done a month earlier. This was more in tune with the Surabayan character, if somewhat unprofessional.

Those families who had lost one of their own were in mourning but after witnessing the spirited response to our ride through some perhaps felt the sacrifices had not been in vain. Hasanuddin wanted to push on to Gresik, 18 kilometers further from Surabaya, but I pointed to the big fuel tank on the Harley, saying it was almost empty. It wasn't. His erratic riding had scared me witless and I was desperate for us to get back safely before it was too dark. We returned exhausted to the compound. We would have been less complacent had we known the British in Jakarta and Singapore were at that moment quietly sending more warships and troops to Surabaya.

8

THE BRITISH ULTIMATUM

MORE BRITISH TROOPS ARRIVE

The *Arek Suroboyo* boys on duty at the harbour awakened on Thursday morning November 1 to the sight of newly arrived British warships. None of us knew the extent of the British reinforcements gathering in the waters off Surabaya harbour but realized that from that day forth every passing day would bring us closer to war. Surabayans started to speak to each other in sombre tones of those sensing a catastrophe would befall them, repeating the phrase *menjelang datangnya badai* (awaiting the hurricane).

The Surabayans' success in removing the British from the occupation of the city at the end of October had greatly influenced our fighters, giving them confidence. They were almost convinced they could defeat the British and Dutch NICA forces and their self-belief had grown after using various weapons in real combat. The older generation and women in the rear lines now also knew their support roles. On the other hand, I knew with certainty that the British would have learned from their defeat and were unlikely to repeat the mistakes in their tactics. After three days of fighting us they had seen beyond the first, raggedy appearance of our fighters and understood how integrated our *Arek Suroboyo* forces were.

After the bitter experience in October the British had signaled they would respond in kind and set about preparing their excuses for a war on Surabayans, the last free citizens in the embryonic Republic, whose future was looking decidedly dim. The British forces that had defeated the powerful Japanese Imperial Army now brought in the cruiser HMS *Sussex* under Rear Admiral Patterson to land 1,500 troops from the destroyers *Carron* and *Cavalier* on 1 November. Major General Mansergh, the new Commander for Surabaya, and Commander of the 5th Indian Division, followed on 3 November with 24,000 troops, armored cars, tanks and squadrons of Mosquito and Thunderbolt fighter-bombers. This was our hurricane in the making.

Since the first of November the British had quietly reassembled the remnants of the Mallaby forces at the harbour. They avoided every possible action that might give rise to incidents while they prepared and consolidated. They were preparing a sudden attack of a military-political-diplomatic nature, but going about it calmly. Almost two weeks would elapse before we knew the true strength of the British land, sea and air forces with which they intended to crush us. They were hoping we had fallen into a state of indifference.

MANSERGH IS CALLED OUT ON AN ATTEMPTED BLUFF

On Wednesday 7 November 1945 the British called our Contact Bureau. They invited Governor Surio and members of the Contact Bureau to meet Major General Mansergh, who had replaced Mallaby. In keeping with their scenarios of secrecy, the meeting would be held at the *Batavia Weg* building, one of the formal conference quarters in the city used especially for top-level meetings. Colonel Pugh and Wing Commander Croon received our Contact Bureau members in a large meeting room.

Major General Mansergh opened the talks:

My name is Major General Mansergh. I am the Commander of the Allied Forces in East Java and represent the Commander of the Allied Forces of Netherlands Indies.

My presence here is to facilitate the repatriation of Allied prisoners of war and former internees and prisoners of other nations, like Swiss, Indian and others, who wish to return home. And also, to disarm the Japanese and repatriate their troops.

The world fully understands that the Allies have the ships and the organization in Surabaya to complete that task and the willingness to help all foreigners seeking repatriation.

Further, they realize that if they are not permitted to return home the responsibility is fully upon all Indonesians. I know there are Swiss and Indian citizens who wish to return home. I am prepared to repatriate them but I am meeting resistance from Indonesia.

It is also widely known to the world that irresponsible armed people have been allowed to pillage and commit murder of unarmed women and children and other uncivilized acts. This happened even after the Allies formally recognized the armed Surabaya Police under Indonesian leadership.

But you gentlemen cannot control the situation.

You have the means but cannot keep law and order.

The world knows of your horrific actions. It had been agreed that several districts of Surabaya were to be occupied by Allied troops and by Indonesians whose task it was to avoid clashes. Your side transgressed, breaking the agreement.

According to the agreement the tanks that now occupy the (Morokrembangan) airfield are to be withdrawn and the Allied forces will occupy the airfield from 1400 hours today. It will be your responsibility if there are further incidents.

Your representatives repeatedly promised guaranteed return of wounded Allied soldiers and prisoners, equipment and trucks and so on. Until now that promise has been late in keeping or totally ignored. I wish to impress upon your gentlemen that I consider you clearly unable or unwilling to keep your promises and honor your guarantees as agreed and that the whole world as well as the Allies know of your failures.

Now I request that the organization of the foreign citizens who wish to be repatriated be continued and that all lost or wounded Allied soldiers, along with trucks, equipment and so on, are quickly returned.

Mansergh waited for Mr Kundan's translation to finish, then sat down.

THE INDONESIAN RESPONSE; CHECKING THE AIRFIELD

The Indonesian party listened to this string of lies while noting the General's arrogance in launching the vulgar accusations. But Governor Surio didn't waver and responded firmly to all the British accusations.

He totally rejected the false claims contained in that document. He said quietly it was not correct that we delayed the evacuation of internees and of those soldiers trapped in several places around Surabaya. The bodies of soldiers that had been found had been returned, along with the wounded. They were brought in on British trucks that were handed over at the same time. We had even given priority to the evacuation of Allied troops and internees. In contrast, the Allies had given priority to transferring "neutral" races such as Indians and Swiss and others, a task totally outside Allied duties. (By that he meant the British were not repatriating the Dutch because they were amassing as supporters for a NICA administration.)

Governor Surio told General Mansergh that the airfield at Morokrembangan would not be surrendered to the Allies. It would remain in our hands. Its status was never discussed with General Mallaby or Naval Colonel Pugh. Nor did he believe that right now there were Indonesian tanks and armored cars in position at the airfield, but as a sign of willingness to cooperate he would send Sudirman and Mohammad to see if the claim of "Indonesian tank and troops and taking up positions" was valid.

The members of the Indonesian delegation saw Major General Mansergh's expression change when he heard what the Governor said about Morokrembangan. The expression indicated the General was surprised. But they were even more annoyed after hearing Mansergh's reaction: "I have documents (saying) that all I said was true and I have my orders."

Pak Surio entrusted Resident Sudirman and Mohammad to make a quick trip to Morokrembangan. Mansergh excused himself, ordering Pugh to continue representing the Allies. Taking his cue, Pak Surio left also, leaving Dul Arnowo and Sungkono to continue discussions with the Allies, which were conducted in high tension. We had rigorously followed the protocol of "pairing" when dealing with the British. If their Commander would not attend a meeting, preferring to send his second-in-command, Governor Surio would deputize Sudirman or Dul Arnowo. When Captain Shaw and Ruslan Abdulgani had been appointed joint secretaries of the Contact Bureau, they met the following day. Ruslan surprised Captain Shaw by appearing in uniform with a Captain's rank, not his usual civvies. Captain Shaw asked:

"Mr Ruslan, I see you are in uniform. How long have you been a soldier?"

"I joined yesterday."

"Just one day and you are already a Captain!"

"You are a Captain, so they said I should be also."

The big difference, as I assessed the pairings, was that Shaw and Abdulgani were civilized, educated and polite men who would in peace time have become natural friends, whereas both Mallaby and Mansergh were unnaturally stiff in their approaches to the Governor, resorting to haughty postures revealing inexperience beyond military training. Abdulgani was not a military man. He had only worn the uniform on instructions from Governor Surio and removed it soon after.

Awaiting Sudirman's return from the airport the Indonesian delegation took the chance to hand over a watch that they thought might be General Mallaby's, found in the burnt out sedan. The meeting was adjourned at ten minutes to two o'clock, the time Mansergh had announced the Allies would begin occupation of the airfield.

All the above information I got from Sungkono, that same afternoon. Now I'll tell you the influence that meeting had on us, Hasanuddin and me, at the time. As I expected, Hasanuddin had begun grumbling about the meeting with the British. He considered it not fitting that General Mansergh invited our Governor to *his* office, especially because the meeting was held on British territory. He thought the General should have come to the Governor's office. Governor Surio represented the central government in Jakarta and several million East Javanese people.

Hasanuddin felt that because the Allies had recognized the Republic of Indonesia in Jakarta, a de facto not de jure recognition, they automatically should recognize the provincial government of East Java. I agreed with him and was in fact disappointed with the Contact Bureau's attitude in responding to the British claims.

But I believed that Surio, Sudirman and Dul Arnowo knew how to deal with their opponents. All three were prominent national *Pergerakan* movement members pre-war. Pak Surio and Pak 'Dirman were prominent in the Parindra Party while Cak Dul was a PNI (Nationalist Party of Indonesia) leader. The Dutch had suspended the Nationalist Party, but it had continued underground activity and still worked with Parindra, which the Dutch had given legal status.

We were proud and pleased to hear Governor Surio's response to the British accusation, but that didn't mean we were less vigilant. Concerning Mansergh's reaction to Pak Surio's answers, Hasanuddin said the General seemed pleased to hear Surio's answer that no Indonesian forces were at the airfield, leading us to think the British had planned to occupy the field.

The senior British military officers accompanying Bung Karno from Jakarta would have viewed the airfield from a military perspective. The presence of thousands of armed fighters greeting the Presidential entourage, and the tense situation, were impressions they would have taken with them. We realized then that Mansergh had mistakenly read from their own intelligence reports when he said he had documents.

The British also knew, from the Japanese leaders who had surrendered to them, the level of Japanese armaments in East Java and that they had trained 70,000 youths for PETA, and, from Major Yamamoto during the surrender talks, may have heard that the East Javanese PETA soldiers were the most truculent and feisty, perhaps even admitting to committing the Blitar mutiny. Christison and Hawthorn could comfortably calculate approximately how many heavy weapons, beach cannons, anti-aircraft guns, and tanks and infantry weapons we possessed. Mansergh was attempting to learn the precise location of these weapons in Surabaya. He had launched a clever, provocative verbal attack, using the situation at Morokrembangan to get a reaction from us. He didn't have time to investigate at ground level. He knew that the Japanese army were experts in camouflage and had passed on that expertise to Indonesians.

BEFORE THE BATTLE FOR SURABAYA

The document General Mansergh had read out was originally dated Saturday 3 November, but that had been crossed out, and 7 November inserted.

Taking into account their previous losses, they may have brought in fighter planes from Singapore or Malaya to ensure the job got done quickly. Perhaps, also, they were politically or diplomatically unprepared in Jakarta. Alternatively, the date change could have been deliberate, intended to inveigle us into feeling more pressured and threatened, a simple form of psychological warfare that can be quite efficient. Given those possibilities we knew we couldn't take our enemy lightly. They had a long and brilliant military history.

Having said that, the people of Surabaya, who possessed no knowledge of British military history, at that moment had no need for it. They knew only that the British were obstructing and tormenting them in their struggle to defend their independence. And not to be forgotten was the fact that they had removed the British occupation troops, in the three-day clash.

Hasanuddin, in one of his angry, anti-British tirades, remarked: "Hario, my young brother-in-arms, the British don't want to recognize our government. That also means they do not recognize our Military Police. Why bother play-acting, wearing these Military Police armbands? Discard the insignia; we'll confront them as ordinary street fighters." His words in principle were facts but I knew there was an element of Surabaya sarcasm in his tone. He surely had not forgotten that before long he would be given the rank of Lieutenant General.

I replied calmly: "Cak Hasan, who said being a Military Policeman was fun? We work not to be judged by Mansergh but to show other nations the independent character of our freedom fighting youth. We all realize we have to keep fighting."

Hasanuddin laughed then scowled at me, saying: "Fuck you! Don't give me lessons. Let's get ready to whack the British."

THE BRITISH CONTEMPTUOUS OF THE REPUBLIC: AREK ANGER

On Thursday morning 8 November we learned from our Military Police unit on security duty with the Contact Bureau that a British courier had delivered a letter to the Governor. It was not addressed to the Governor of East Java but to Mr. R. M. T. A. Surio. This meant that the British were emphasizing their lack of recognition of both the Republic and the status of Governor Surio as Governor of East Java.

The letter contained, among other things, allegations that Surabaya was occupied by looters and that Surio had failed to carry out agreements and promises, had delayed the evacuation of nationals desirous of leaving, and had prevented the disarmament of Japanese forces. Therefore, the British would enter the town and disarm the lawless mobs. The crowning insult, at the end of the letter was Mansergh's demand that "Mr. Surio" come to the *Batavia Weg* the next morning, Friday 9 November 1945 at 11.00 hours precise to receive further instructions.

The Governor instructed the secretary of the Contact Bureau, Ruslan Abdulgani, and the interpreter, Kundan, to respond in English, using the Dutch spellings of '*Sourabaya, Soerio and Madoera*':

Major General
R. C. Mansergh
Commander Allied Land Forces
East Java, Sourabaya

Sir,

I have for acknowledgement your two letters...the second dated 8th November 1945, No.G-512-2, addressed to Mr. R. M. T.A. Soerio, who incidentally, I may tell you, is the Governor of East Java, and I think and must kindly request you to please address all official correspondence to me with more decorum.

I expect it from you as representative of the Commander-in-Chief of the Allied Forces to conduct all personal meetings in a more friendly and unbiased attitude of mind. I shall be more obliged if you will kindly realise that you are in the East charged with a solemn and sacred duty, and until you meet me in a more sincere and friendly spirit, all further communications between us must, by virtue of your attitude, be conducted by letter.

1. In connection with clause 1 of you last letter...we are continuing with all our efforts to fulfill our part of the agreement.
2. Regarding clause 2...your version of the state of affairs in Sourabaya is not correct...if you can (see looting, or otherwise) I shall be glad to go into such matters immediately.
3. Concerning the delay in transferring nationals from individual areas to Tanjung Perak, I may point out this is not caused by any other reason except a personally hesitant attitude and lack of proper preparations by individual nationals.
4. I may bring to your kind notice that Major-General Hawthorn never used the words "Netherlands East Indies" but uses instead the words "Java, Madoera, Bali and Lombok."
5. Normal conditions of law and order prevail at the moment.
6. Regarding the sixth clause...I am anxious to know the necessity for the allied Forces to enter the town and the neighbourhood of Sourabaya and other areas of East Java when the agreement concluded between Major General Hawthorn and President Dr Sukarno mentioned that only two places, i.e. Darmo and Tanjung Perak will be guarded by Allied Forces and that as soon as the internees and RAPWI people are withdrawn from Darmo, the forces would also move to Tanjung Perak.The question of your forces entering the town of Sourabaya is neither advisable nor conducive to peace and harmony...I have no doubt that a sympathetic attitude towards our difficult task coupled with patience will avoid unnecessary misunderstanding on both sides.
7. I sincerely hope that you will work with us in the spirit of goodwill and friendship realizing our difficulties with vision and foresight,

and have no doubts that such harmony will be conducive to a solution of your difficulties.

I thank you in anticipation,
Yours faithfully,
M. T. O. Soerio,
Governor of East Java

Governor Surio had reminded Mansergh that even his own Commander did not use the term "Netherlands Indies" but "Java, Madura, Lombok and Bali," that there had been no incidents since the agreement between Hawthorn and Sukarno and, that he saw no compelling need for the British to enter Surabaya while there was an agreement that they could only occupy Darmo and Tanjung Perak. Surio warned General Mansergh not to enter Surabaya because it would have a negative influence on law and order and said this would destroy all the good work that had been achieved with Colonel Pugh in searching for a peaceful outcome.

But General Mansergh wanted his day in the sun as a general. It seemed likely that he had already prepared his Ultimatum for war. We learned he had prepared a document he would hand over to the Police Chief, head of Radio Surabaya, and other prominent leaders, but went into a rage when we had sent a courier as our envoy, to whom he handed the document.

THE ULTIMATUM

To all Indonesians of Surabaya:
On October 28th, 1945, Indonesians of Surabaya treacherously and without provocation, suddenly attacked the British Forces who had come with the purpose of disarming and concentrating the Japanese Forces, of bringing relief to Allied prisoners of war and internees, and of maintaining law and order. In the fighting which ensued, British personnel were killed or wounded, some are missing, interned women and children were massacred, and finally Brigadier Mallaby was foully murdered when trying to implement the truce, which had been broken in spite of Indonesian undertakings.
The above crimes against civilisation cannot go unpunished.

Unless, therefore, the following orders are obeyed without fail by 06.00 hours on 10th November at the latest, I shall enforce them with all the sea, land and air forces at my disposal, and those Indonesians who have failed to obey my orders will be solely responsible for the bloodshed which must inevitably ensue.

(Signed) Maj. Gen. R. C. Mansergh
Commander Allied Land Forces, East Java.

EAST JAVA GOVERNOR SURIO REJECTS THE ULTIMATUM

In previous demands on the Governor, eight types and makes of weapons were to be handed in. They included not only pistols, rifles, cannon, tanks, mortar, grenades and the like, but also spears, swords, keris, sharpened bamboo and poisoned arrows, indicating the effectiveness of basic weapons adroitly used were a concern to them.

The British Ultimatum and other pamphlets were dropped by plane over Surabaya around one o'clock in the afternoon. Perhaps they were thinking that form of psychological warfare would be sufficient to break the spirit of the *Arek Suroboyo*. The Ultimatum had the opposite effect. The hatred the people felt towards the British and Dutch intensified.

In response to the Ultimatum by Major General Mansergh, the leaders of the People's Security Army invited leaders of all 66 of our combat bodies in Surabaya City, to their headquarters that afternoon. Their compound was situated in Pregolan, an elite area during the Dutch times. The luxury homes in the area had been occupied by upper-level Dutch colonial employees and business people, before the Japanese arrived. The old historic kampungs of Tegalsari, Pelemahan, Kampung Malang, Kedungdoro, Kedung Klinter, Kaliasin, Keputran, all densely populated, still encircled the district.

At the meeting that afternoon the youth leaders from all those kampungs gathered in the yard and on the street in front of the Pregolan residence that had been converted to TKR headquarters.

SURABAYA-WIDE PREPARATIONS FOR WAR

War was in the air, though we remained calm, and our expressions were not those of wasteful belligerence. The hurricane clouds were gathering. We all carried our weapons that had now become permanent extensions to our new magnified *personas* as genuine revolutionaries; rifles and automatic weapons like Sten-guns and side arms, and at the minimum, several hand grenades each. It was scarcely believable that this whole section of our juvenile society, not yet 18 years old, so innocent and deprived until few weeks earlier, were now gathering as confident, upright young adults dreaming of a freedom that until now had existed for them as imagery in *wayang* shadow play legends.

The marginally older leaders or unit commanders all wore pistols but were otherwise indistinguishable from the school-aged majority. The average age of those at this historic gathering was around 22 years. Many were just 15 or so years of age, boys already skilled in weapon handling and explosives, and a dozen or more of whom had never previously sat inside a motor vehicle were now competent drivers of jeeps and trucks or rode the motorcycles we used as for courier work between combat units.

Our uniforms were various and incomplete, our footwear ranged from boots confiscated from the Japanese down to flimsy rubber sandals. Some of us had longish hair, but most wore it normal length and others had it very short, almost bald, following the shaved-head trend enforced on students by the Japanese. Our weapons were clean, and always handy to us, and we carried ammunition in belts or strapped to us.

In later years, artists wishing to conjure up a golden era they would never themselves experience, erroneously depicted us in combat uniform, weapons raised as we stood in bold, heroic poses that allowed our long hair to flow from under useless headbands. But we had no need for headbands or mock, aggressive poses, and long hair and beards were rare during the Japanese occupation. We were gathered on serious business, with fashion or posturing playing no part in this life or death contract we were entering into to win independence.

THE MERDEKA ATAU MATI DECLARATION SIGNED

The gathering of 66 units representing thousands of fighters unanimously chose Sungkono as Commander of Surabaya City Defense and Surachman as Battle Commander. The meeting of *pemuda* (youth) leaders also set three defense lines for the city:

1. all Pasar Babakan Road
2. the Pasar Besar viaduct
3. the southernmost line was the Wonokromo district

The meeting also unanimously resolved to swear an oath around the *"Merdeka atau Mati"* call, which ran as follows:

> *Forever Free!*
> *The Sovereignty of the Indonesian State and Indonesian People proclaimed on 17 August 1945 we faithfully swear to defend; collectively responsibly, united, we are willing to sacrifice ourselves, committing to Freedom or Death.*
> *Now free, forever free.*
> *Surabaya, 9 November 1945.*
> *At 18.46 hours.*

This extraordinary document was signed just 12 hours before the British launched their 10 November offensive. The oath, the record of the meeting, and the calm in which it was conducted gave lie to the British claims that we were an uncontrolled mob of looters, armed and vicious, running amok with bloodlust.

This was a "prepare to fight" document, written by very young men largely from underprivileged upbringings, whose parents and relatives in their tiny kampung dwellings were organizers of combat kitchens, first aid posts and couriers. Even the white-haired, frail kampung elders had turned to laboring to fortify defense posts and road blocks by dragging in furniture and old iron, or stitching large camouflage nets in preparation for the looming British onslaught.

At the end of the meeting Sungkono gave a brief, impressive declaration that was far more influential than a hundred raging radio speeches.

Brothers,
I want to defend the city of Surabaya. Surabaya cannot be left to face the danger without us.
If any of you wish to leave and abandon the city, I will not prevent you. But I will myself defend the city you have abandoned.

None of us left the city. We stayed to fight.

THE BRITISH FINISH UP THEIR HUMANITARIAN DUTIES

The British had prepared well. They had used the ceasefire to complete their humanitarian duties, hurriedly transferring vulnerable civilian internees and prisoners-of-war out of the city to remove them from harm's way and exposure to hostage taking. The British forces needed unhindered access to Surabaya's wide boulevards and major buildings where their enemy, the Indonesian "insurgents," would be at a disadvantage, especially against tanks. Reinstating the Dutch would have to wait!

SURIO REJECTS THE ULTIMATUM, NIGHT OF 9 NOV

That evening Governor Surio, Resident Sudirman and the Chairman of the Independence Committee, Dul Arnowo gathered in the small hotel Pension Marijke in Embong Sawo to discuss the dangerous situation now that all the diplomatic efforts with the British had failed.

As East Java's most senior leaders, they contacted the Central Government leaders in Jakarta, requesting their response to the British Ultimatum. Jakarta's agreement to a ceasefire had left Surabayans vulnerable by giving the British time to rearm and ship in massive reinforcements, at a time when we had the upper hand.

THE JAKARTA GOVERNMENT ABDICATES RESPONSIBILITY

At 2200 hours the Central government in Jakarta, via the Minister for Foreign Affairs, answered with a lame reply, reiterating that the British officers of the Supreme Allied Command in Jakarta had decided to use force the next day, 10 November 1945, if the people of Surabaya did not heed the Ultimatum.

The Jakarta Central Government added that they would leave the decision, to obey the Ultimatum or to fight it, to Surabayans themselves. Ruslan Abdulgani was to exclaim: "What sort of answer was this? Not to answer the question is not a decision!" After receiving the Central Government's message, Governor Surio discussed the situation with other leaders, but not using the telephone lines. They concluded that all Surabayans would honor the sacred oaths and were prepared to fight the British for their independence.

GOVERNOR SURIO'S HISTORIC NIGHT-TIME RADIO ADDRESS

Governor Surio went on air at 2300 hours with his historic radio address to hundreds of thousands of Surabayans and East Javanese gathered around rare radio sets at an hour when normally most of them would have long been asleep. A crowd of several hundred had quietly gathered in the dark outside Radio Surabaya to hear a relay of the speech on external loudspeakers. The people listened in an extraordinary silence, uttering not a sound until Surio had finished the speech. For years to come, I could still recall his lines:

Brothers, all our efforts to negotiate were in vain. The Central Government has entrusted Surabayans to decide the matter before us.

We must now have the courage to confront all challenges in order to defend our independence.

We have repeatedly said that we would prefer total destruction to again being colonized.

Now, in confronting the English Ultimatum, we must hold fast to that belief.

We are standing firm. We refuse the terms of the Ultimatum.

When we face tomorrow and all that it may bring, let us hold firmly to our unity; unity of government, of our Defense Forces, Police, and the united powers of our youth and ordinary people.

We ask the All-Powerful One to grant us the inner strength and the blessings of the Almighty in our coming battle.

Selamat berjuang! Stay safe in combat!

His speech was reinforced by an emotive, fiery Bung Tomo speech over Rebel Radio that could be heard on all public radios in town as well as overseas via the RRI short wave.

That same night of 9 November 1945 the *Arek Suroboyo* of the People's Security Corps in Pregolan Road together set the defensive front line. They also divided the city of Surabaya into three defense sectors: East, Central and West. I was impressed by the extent of the progress we had all made in patching together forces that ten weeks ago were at best an optimistic plan, for boys with no weapons, no structure and amorphous leadership, who were fuelled by a burning ambition to be free.

The Eastern Defense Sector, called simply the Eastern Line, covered a long list of districts to be defended by our new Navy Corps and many strategic kampung areas east of the Kali Mas as it drained into the port. There were 25 combat units, including one under the Hizbullah banner.

The Central Defense Sector covered the most famous place names in Surabaya's nineteenth- and twentieth-century history: Jembatan Merah (Red Bridge:), The Post Office, the Viaduct, Railway Road, Semut Station, Turi Market, and the districts on the banks of the Kali Mas, Tanjungan, Kaliasin, Darmo, Simpang and Wonokromo. This sector had 22 separate Combat Corps.

Our Western Sector had 19 Combat forces to defend a broad expanse. The decisions as to geographic placement were made in an atmosphere I find difficult to describe. Tension, optimism and enthusiasm, powered our emotions as we gathered at Pregolan that evening. Words seemed inadequate to describe the scene. I was carried along in this atmosphere, which began for me when I was helping our recruits dig defensive trenches in front of our own compound in Pasar Besar. While digging, the boys on watch at the harbour came to report the unnerving news that more British warships had been seen arriving at Tanjung Perak harbor.

My rational, or should I say "intellectual" thinking, told me that it would be difficult to defend our compound against a British offensive because of its configuration and location, but the boys digging the trenches alongside me had declared they would hold out "until the last drop of blood." Finally, my rational approach was wrestled aside by emotions and enthusiasm, and I daringly agreed with them.

We had just a few hours to prepare. We stopped telephoning each other to ask about logistics or the chain of command, feeling we had done all what we could and did not wish to express doubt. The complex strategies we had devised were now compressed into a battle cry: "Freedom or Death! Merdeka atau Mati!"

No one let the fear of the enemy's obvious superior strength deter us, nor did we agonize over our own shortcomings and inexperience. Perhaps unconsciously we had decided that it was too late now for such computations.

Nevertheless, we still had to fight the enemy next morning. The October fighting had taught us many valuable lessons. Among them were that the "kampung mothers" (*Ibu-Ibu Kampung*) now understood the importance of supporting the fighters with combat kitchens, first aid help and moral support in the events about to unfold. We had supplied kitchens with food from raids on Japanese granaries that yielded rice, corn, flour and other foodstuffs they had kept secretly for themselves. We were the 'looters' the British referred to, not caring to learn that we had distributed the food back to our own people.

CONTINUING PREPARATIONS FOR WAR

Another lesson learned was to test the operation of important weapons like the anti-aircraft guns the Japanese had left us. The British had managed to sabotage our cannon during the ceasefire, and we had not noticed because the weapons all appeared in good condition. After that experience, we removed all our big guns to safer locations.

The evening of 9 November 1945 was an important, historic moment. The event was the merger of Surabayans in spirit, soul and strength in their determination to confront the enemy, given voice in the *"Merdeka atau Mati"* call, a spirit immeasurable to an enemy like General Mansergh who said he would "thrash" the people of Surabaya. The British experts on psychological warfare who had drawn up the British Ultimatum, using threats and an order to surrender, clearly misjudged the expected response to their work. They sought to divide a united people, but the Ultimatum had the opposite effect of consolidation and increased determination.

The line-up of our formal forces after that momentous evening I had memorized thoroughly, perhaps to reinforce my own unit's position or simply to gather confidence in our mission by reviewing how far we had all come in short weeks in organizing a resistance force.

- 8 Battalions of People's Security Corps (BKR)

- 4 Battalions of Naval Corps (PSF).

- 2 Battalions of Combined Police Forces (PI/PPI/CSP).

- 1 Battalion of the Students Army (TKR)

- 15 Battalions of Indonesian Youth Corps (PRI)

- 1 Battalion of another youth group (BPRI)

- 1 Battalion of Hizbullah

We had 32 Battalions comprising about 30,000 men who had trained with the Japanese PETA or Heiho auxiliary forces. That was the foundation of our national Army, decreed just a few weeks earlier on Friday 5 October. In other parts of Java there were

40,000 more PETA men, but they would only be of use to the Republic if Surabaya held out.

PETA training was far short of professional, and the equipment and weapons were sub-standard. Hasanuddin had been a senior PETA officer, whereas I had added private military tuition, including the art and science of warfare the Japanese would never have given me. Our popular military leader Colonel Sungkono had risen to the highest PETA rank in East Java, earning scrutiny from the Japanese who correctly suspected his loyalty, particularly after the Blitar mutiny.

Our battalions had around 400 men, but could range to 800, whereas traditional battalions usually comprised 1,200 to 1,300 men. We estimated the kampung street fighters numbered more than five times the size of the formal battalions. They had been the real power in our weapon raids on the Japanese, seizing sufficient weapons to arm more than 140,000 fighters, with varying equipment. We also had special squads of just 15, or others up to 100, depending on their geographic origins, and compact, mobile groups with freelancers the French called *Franc-tireurs* (snipers), that had personalized leadership.

The teenagers opted to stay in squads with their childhood friends from the kampungs or school friends, and felt more comfortable going into battle with their own kampung leaders. The system of kampung volunteers choosing leaders from within their own ranks had begun during the September weapons seizures and was now well tested.

We expected intense street fighting where our kampung boys originated, for they knew every meter of pathways and lanes, every shortcut, every contour and bend, to hamper a British advance. The British, however, would be superior in warfare on open ground with their trained infantry and modern tanks that could dash down our wide boulevards with ease.

9

THE BATTLE FOR SURABAYA

DAY ONE: Saturday 10 November

Before daybreak on Saturday 10 November our Commander of the Surabaya Defense, Colonel Sungkono, toured the city calling at as many posts as he could manage to check on their preparedness.

He was a quiet, thoughtful man, who pre-war had continued undaunted by several arrests and detention for nationalist activities during the Dutch time. When he arrived at our Military Police compound he simply asked: "Are you ready?" (*Sudah siap?*)

Hasanuddin answered for both of us: "All ready." (*Siap!*) Sungkono smiled to indicate he both understood and was satisfied and went into the dark night to continue his inspection tour. The unspoken question in the famous *Siap* call was: "Are you prepared to die for our freedom?" We all understood the coded question, so we gave a loud, longer answer: "*Siiiii-aaaaap!*"

What else was there to say? Deep down were aware that none of us had sufficient military expertise to enable us to face an invasion by a modern army. More talk was unnecessary. We knew it was now a matter of Freedom or Death, *Merdeka atau Mati!*

DATANGNYA BADAI: THE HURRICANE ARRIVES

The 'hurricane' arrived at 0600 hours, rolling in from the bay with a thunderous roar. The British had launched a massive land, sea and air assault they called a Punitive Operation. The difference between this and their previous, botched occupation of the city was that they opened by attacking our forces in the northern sector. They began shelling from warships and coordinated their mortar fire with terrifying and repeated aerial bombardment of explosives and incendiaries.

They inflicted us with a constant barrage of shells, bombs and strafing from *Thunderbolt* and *Mosquito* fighter-bombers they had secretly brought down from Singapore for the Surabaya assault, and sent tanks into battle to cover to their famous British-Indian infantry. In the first hours they moved systematically inland from their base at the harbour to hold the dock areas and Tanjung Perak harbor and a segment of northern Surabaya.

It was an assault of bombing and artillery fire that in Europe during World War II was carried out by two modern armies confronting each other. But when inflicted upon a densely inhabited city in a land where a state of war did not exist, it could may well be categorized as "uncivilized", an accusation the Allies frequently made against the Germans. The shelling startled our young men who had never before heard anything so devastating, forcing them to take cover. They soon recovered and were sufficiently coping with the shelling by the time the infantry confronted us.

The early British advance soon slowed at every kampung and progressed in short bursts, finally being blocked around the Gresik Road and at Kebalen, East Kalimas, Nyamplungan, and Pegirikan. Our men appeared to be waiting calmly. We had placed a squad outside the compound, near the Flora Cinema situated to our west on Bubutan Street, as a reserve force.

One TKR Company under Commander Ridwan was placed along the elevated railway line to the viaduct that was situated between the north of our building and across the road. A few days earlier I had, in fact, discussed with Hasanuddin the use of the railway line as a defensive position. Ridwan placed heavy artillery positions on the railway line, using papaya trees propped up as "camouflage," but I warned him that if he could see the British, they could see him, and even they were unlikely to believe that papaya trees grew on our railway tracks!

There soon came to us from the Tanjung Perak harbour a thunderous noise like that of empty drums thrown from a truck, soon realizing it was the sound of heavy artillery on the move. Hasanuddin was grumbling because he had no news from the front line to our north. We had no field telephones or other modern communications and none of our couriers brought news. We were in the Central Defensive area under the Command of Kretarto *Pak Kret*. We waited on maximum alert. Meanwhile, the sound of the cannon and mortar was getting closer, but still no reports from Kretarto's units. Where were their command posts? We were already very aware that this combat was nothing like the fighting we had experienced in October.

THE BRITISH WAR MACHINE ADVANCES

The enemy advanced by using their artillery to clear the path forward. Civilians from kampungs began to slip away, heading south, away from the fighting. Those departing were elderly or mothers carrying infants and leading young children. Some among them were already wounded, but there was no panic; they moved as in a dream. Those scenes and their plight had a great effect upon me, angering me and stirring my revolutionary zeal. The retaliations from the kampung fighters along Gresik Road halted the British advance after three hours, slowing down the fighting in Kebalen, East Kalimas, Nyamplungan, and Pegirikan.

We then heard from afar the sequences of heavy artillery fire; that of aircraft sounded closer. Hasanuddin and Ridwan were beside me, perhaps in a similar state of emotional turmoil. We were each convinced we had to take action and not simply wait around. To hell with the forward defense line we had drawn yesterday!

Orderly, rapid action across the front was out of the question because we had no radio networks to coordinate an attack. We decided our entire corps would do better if split into smaller companies, each of around 10 or 12 men, and each with a single purpose. The purpose that had shaped our combined thought: to seek and kill the enemy.

Hasanuddin ordered me to gather the troops to instruct them along these search-and-kill lines, replacing the waiting game. We had to adapt ourselves to the new conditions of warfare and not to follow the Japanese style of orderly company and battalion structure they called *Sidokang*.

Our new field of fighting now included kampungs, roads and narrow streets and alleyways that twisted and turned. The kampung defenders ahead of us to the north were fighting to the death. They were bombarded, burned, trampled and harassed and had only their steely determination and light weapons to defend themselves. They became crazed, amok.

The British bombers were circling, their loud engines reverberating above us, their pilots and navigators directing their artillery and mortar fire by radio to ground crews. Modern warfare had arrived and was flattening the town.

Suddenly, we heard loud shellfire blasting from behind our compound. What the hell? Where did we get that 4 mm cannon? We were astonished to see that some of our ammunition carriers had physically dragged a massive artillery piece into the middle of the road and were aiming the long barrel into the sky above us, to use as an anti-aircraft gun against a prowling plane. The boys had tied bamboo poles to each of the gun's three-pronged stand to lift it while the dedicated shooter fired standing up, using it as an anti-aircraft weapon against the light planes the British used as forward control, spotter planes.

Several boys were feeding shells into the cannon to keep it firing. Who had ordered them to go into action and where they learned to use that artillery piece was something I needn't know just then. But they got the job done. The plane's engine noise abated as it drifted out of our range.

I shouted to gather the troops for new orders. Shell explosions boomed around the post office, 300 meters west of our compound. Hasanuddin stood in front of the troops whom I had waiting on alert, facing the Governor's office. They were at the ready and I did not want to disperse because Hasanuddin had to shout loudly to counter the noise from the bombardments, saying there was now no need to defend our compound. We were clearly vulnerable. We would henceforth fight to defend our independence!

We would move from our present command post to the left bank of the Kali Mas in the Peneleh kampung, a new strategy. There was already a second command post arranged on the right bank in Kedung Doro kampung near the former Dutch *Melkbrun* dairy. We instructed each of these companies to act independently. It was time for us to take action up to the enemy, not wait for them to come to us. Hasanuddin spoke to the men in his fervent manner. His short, muscled frame appeared tense as he spoke; he then raised his fists and shouted, "Merdeka! Freedom!"

Meanwhile the shells were pounding in regular rhythm, and the explosions were getting closer. The trees around us were shaking and their branches shook and dropped as though cut through with a sharp blade, as the flying shrapnel struck. A shell burst on the road close to our compound and in the same moments shells began raining down on the Governor's office and forecourt, sending up a spray of stones and dust from the asphalt. Then rifle bullets struck near us and several of our men flattened themselves for cover, including Iskak, one of the teenagers with us from the Praban and Ketabang Middle High School.

Hasan moved inside the building and at that moment, just as I paced toward the head of the troops out front, the building was bombarded with artillery fire, sending some boys running past me. But they were not my men! Ridwan's men on the railway track had taken a direct hit, just before our own building was struck, and were taking cover. I had time only to shout, "Tiaraap!

Get down!" *All*, including Ridwan's men, lay in prone defensive positions.

I don't know how long we lay there as shells exploded around us. The ground shook and the air was filled with the stink of TNT. I crawled around, lifting my head to look back at the building when I heard the threatening sound of a plane engine and saw oil drums in the rear of our compound burst into fire, sending up thick black smoke. I could see through the front main window a figure of someone standing with arms raised, screaming. Several seconds later, a torrent of shells rained down on the building and the figure with raised arms disappeared from view. Another blast blinded me and I fell unconscious.

When I came to I was almost flat on my back. The shelling had continued relentlessly, and seemed to be edging toward us again. At my feet the two friends, Iskak and Iswahyudi, were still lying prone. Iskak was Catholic, Iswahyudi Moslem. They had grown up together and were the closest of friends in life, and were now praying aloud for their lives, faces flat to the earth, using High Javanese!

I felt blood from small wounds congealing on my neck and behind my ear. Splattered on my back and uniform was something sticky and porridge-like. I wiped it off with my hand; it was human brain. I stood and carefully looked around; not far from me was a headless body.

When the shelling seemed to edge away from us, others stood and moved, but were dizzy. The various squad captains gathered their troops, calling them to move around. Several bodies were stretched out, never to move again. During a lull in the shelling we buried our dead in the Military Police Compound. (Fifty years later, when machines were digging up the foundations for the Heroes' Monument in the heart of Surabaya, several human bones and weapons were uncovered, and I knew with certainty they were the remains of our men killed on that first day of the Battle.)

Hasanuddin emerged from the building, telling me the obvious: our headquarters had been destroyed. "There are several bodies scattered around but I have no idea who they are," he said, meaning they were now unrecognizable. More shells passed over our head, screaming in their trajectory. They were now targeting Bubutan and Kranggan districts south of us.

Ridwan suddenly appeared. After seeing me bleeding he called one of his men to bring a small towel over to wipe the blood off. He quickly said: "We weren't strong enough to hold out against their shelling, but the boys are back at their positions now. Ah...that's our artillery, we're starting to return fire. I'm going back."

He quickly left us, but the burst of fire was in fact not from his men but a low flying fighter. I had never doubted the flimsy papaya tree 'camouflage' on the rail lines would be quickly dealt with.

Hasan' pointed to the rear of our compound shouting: "Warn the boys at the Flora cinema!" I saw what he meant. I ran, with Iskak and several other troops, to our reserves squad's post near the Flora cinema. On the street we encountered two women and an old man who, at first, I thought was carrying a baby. But he was actually holding in his arms a bundle of his entrails spilling from a deep stomach wound. One of the young men with me vomited at this sight.

The road was littered with rubble, and snapped power lines were dangling free. Several bodies were splayed on the footpath. The British had blown up Hasanuddin's car. The driver's door had been ripped open. Close by I saw a man crawling painfully and as I approached he looked at me and slowly lifted his arm and said to me, "Merdeka! Merdeka!...Young Sir". It was Hasanuddin's driver. His knee was smashed and the bone protruded.

Providentially, a group of Red Cross workers headed by Dr Suwondo came to help. I considered staying to help victims, but quickly discarded the idea in favor of combat action. The British had brought this on and it was the *British* who had to be destroyed.

That was my recall of the first day's fighting in the Battle for Surabaya, after the British had brought in their big artillery guns as cover for their troops. The following days were a repeat of the first, but by the end of the first few days we had become familiar with the sound shocks of ship-to-shore shelling, artillery fire, aerial bombardment and strafing, and the deadly clank of tank tracks heralding the arrival of the infantry. Their columns of infantrymen's boots stamping on asphalt in the wake of their tanks were an ominous sight as they progressed steadily down the wide, once-beautiful boulevards of our city.

AFTER 10 NOVEMBER: STREET FIGHTERS JOIN FORMAL UNITS

After the intense British shelling from offshore and mortar barrage on the morning of the first day of the Battle on 10 November, the *Arek* kampung fighters merged with more formal units of the People's Security Army, or the fledgling Navy, or a massive unit known as Republican Youth (PRI) and Hizbullah and others, where they got more guidance in their tenacious fight to hold off the British advance.

Since the morning of Sunday 11 November the British troops, along with their skilled Gurkha units, had gone into action protected by artillery and tanks. The fighting extended into our suburbs of Semampir, Sawah Pulo, Sawah Kurung, Jatipuro, Sidotopo and Nyamplungan, where Ruslan Abdulgani's family lived, and they showered bombs on what they considered were our key defensive areas in the Great Marketplace (Pasar Besar), the Post Office and the Red Bridge (Jembatan Merah).

THE BRITISH ADVANCE IS SLOWED; THEY INTENSIFY BOMBING

The British, according to news reports from their military command in Jakarta, had predicted the people of Surabaya would be "on their knees" after the opening days of artillery fire and bombing. There was a second news release quoting the British Command "expressing surprise after meeting such stiff resistance" when they had not taken the city after a week of intense bombardment. Their infantry had at first used batteries of heavy mortar on the kampungs closest to their base in the northern harbor area, and panzers to advance, winning a lot of early ground that gave them confidence. But the panzers were ineffective against the agile street fighters moving in and around the kampungs.

The panzers also quickly ran out of ammunition and were a soft target for the rapid-strike boys using hand grenades and clamping magnetic mines on the vehicles, putting the British at their mercy. But the British soon altered their tactics to limit losses, and for every day they were halted there was another in which they took ground from us.

Perhaps it was because the British could see how many hundreds of new volunteers were arriving daily to help us, fearing the numbers would never end, that alerted us to the mix in attitudes the British were exhibiting as the Battle dragged on, the obvious one being their displeasure in how well we were holding on. There was also the widely known international condemnation from India, Egypt, the US and Australia for their treatment of the people of Surabaya. Wire service reports our leaders had picked up on short wave radio referred also to complaints from London politicians that Britain was "draining its treasury in a military adventure" being conducted months after their men should have been safely back home. The leading advocates of independence for India, Jawaharlal Nehru and Muhammad Jinnah, called for Indian troops to be withdrawn from the conflict against Indonesians fighting for self-rule. The longer we held out, the better our chances of succeeding in swinging world opinion against the British and the Dutch.

OFFSHORE SHELLING

The one certain sign that the British were only out for revenge was their use of offshore shelling from warships, firing at positions four to six kilometers ahead of their farthest advanced troops, which could only have the effect of general destruction and casualties on fleeing civilians. It had taken us several days to become immune to the fearful screaming of massive shells above us, the noise bringing confusion and doubt as to where they might land. The civilians, especially the children, were in constant fear of shells and bombing until they were well clear of city limits and on the way into the safety of rural East Java. Once past the southern limits they were safe from the bombers that could not reach far inland because of their limited fuel tanks.

Along the way we had successfully launched numerous counter moves, often spontaneous, unplanned attacks driven by sheer determination and the restated goal of killing the enemy. The apparently coordinated timing of these counter attacks would in normal military theory be considered a planned reprisal, but that was not so. They were coincidental or fortuitous. These reprisals, when apparently on the verge of defeat in some area, were later described by a British military tactical expert as "never-ending waves despite running into a great barrage of gunfire", without realizing that the "waves" were not the same troops from the companies they had first locked in combat. Both the street fighters and the Security Forces attacked hour after hour, but the repeat waves were in fact new personnel, similarly attired and armed, replacing large numbers who had fallen in previous waves. In these horrific firefights the losses on both sides were heavy, and ours sometimes horrendous, with men climbing over fallen comrades to continue the attacks.

We had more collateral losses also, because so many of our civilians not directly involved in the battle and were often cut down by stray bullets, falling victim during firefights with the British. The street fighters truly proved their commitment to their precious motto of "one falls, a thousand rise." In battle others quickly replaced the fighters killed or wounded behind them, enabling us to keep constant numbers confronting the enemy. The British troops were made to feel they were facing endless waves of armed street fighters.

By night, our young fighters had considerable successes using 81-mm mortars when shooting at visible targets. They preferred moving in darkness because they could get close to the enemy to effectively sight their weapons, whereas their effectiveness in looping, parabolic mortar fire at unseen targets was poor, for they had no training in calculating trajectories. Another favored weapon was the *tekidanto* – a grenade launcher they called the "little mortar." Several boys were skilled with this weapon and by using its parabolic trajectory they were able to hit enemies within a 100-meter radius. The weapon was easily carried in one hand and needed no supporting equipment. We had a stockpile of original Japanese grenades to fit them and they became a nightmare for the British.

THE BRITISH BOMBERS STRIKE AND DESTROY OUR COMPOUND

Our PTKR Military Police compound near the Governor's office got another pounding. It seemed the British thought our Military Police HQ was the main headquarters for the People's Security Army, a view they may have gained when they first went into the city on Friday 26 October, driving on the road past our compound. The impressive, luxurious building then housed our uniformed troops, and clearly visible machine-gun posts out front may have cemented that impression.

We were also an ideal target for warships at sea, for opposite us was the tall bell tower of Government House, visible from the harbour. The British clearly saw our headquarters as an easy target for destruction. The building was so thoroughly damaged it could not be rebuilt. After the war it was completely razed and on its grounds the Tugu Pahlawan (Heroes Monument) now stands.

THE WAR RAGES ON: CLOSE FIGHTING; SLOW ADVANCE

The conflict in the old town, where the narrow streets twisted and turned among densely inhabited kampungs, favored our style of door-to-door fighting, but left the buildings in a mess. The British army was perhaps unfamiliar with cities not neatly set out in blocks and easily lost their way, especially at night and without street maps.

Volunteer fighters from outside Surabaya equally suffered difficulties. Accidental confrontations occurred among our troops, unavoidable during such close encounters. The British, with a good radio network, were able to easily direct *their* forces. When they knew there was a blockage on the left flank, they simply sent new directions by radio. For example, in one clash they redirected their tanks and panzers via the *Batavische Weg* and turned east and attacked us in the Sidotopo, Kapasan and surrounds. Our original assault had seriously damaged them and they correctly reasoned that if the lines to *Bataviasche Weg* were broken they would be unable to bring in their tanks and panzers.

The enemy put enormous pressure on us, forcing us to skirt around the eastern districts of Kenjeran Road and Ngaglik. The people living in the old kampungs of Sidotopo, Semut and Ngaglik, were poor and simple people who somehow managed to defend their territory for three days and nights.

Bung Tomo's Rebel Radio broadcasts were now being relayed throughout Java and picked up as far south as Australia and as far north as Thailand, with the result that international pressures were mounting on the British and Dutch to halt their advance, and perhaps more importantly, led to the outbreak of passionate vocal, physical and material support for us. An appeal for medical help brought hundreds of volunteer nurses and a good number of skilled doctors. Another appeal for food brought an inundation into the Wonokromo station, which for most of the time was out of reach of the British bombardments.

K'tut Tantri, whom the British called 'Surabaya Sue', was the adopted name of Muriel Pearson, a 47-year-old Glasgow-born, US-trained artist who had lived several years in Bali until jailed by the Japanese on charges of spying. She was moved to a Surabaya jail where she was tortured until she was released following the surrender. Tantri helped the independence cause with her production of Rebel Radio reports in English, giving the world our side of the story. The more help we could get the more likely we could convince the world of our cause.

Bung Tomo's *Radio Pemberontakan* was now an indispensable weapon in our fight against the British. Listeners waited for the 'Tiger Shark' signature tune that led into his battle speeches: "Fellow Indonesian youths throughout the country, especially those who are now on the battlefield in Surabaya: Many of our friends have died. Blood has flowed in this city. Many of your friends will never come home...But, believe me, the flesh, blood, and bones of those who died will one day fertilize an independent country, where their children will enjoy equal prosperity and justice... Allahu Akbar! Merdeka!"

The Tiger Shark introduction was the signal for us to take a deep breath and listen. Listeners looked for hidden codes in the Tiger Shark instrumental but the truth was that the Japanese had destroyed all the Western music they could find in the Radio station's record library, but somehow missed this Hawaiian tune. Tiger Shark brought out emotional responses, more acute and heartfelt as the fighting dragged on and our casualties mounted.

CHINESE SNIPERS: DANGER FROM OUR REAR LINES

Midway through the Battle we were forced to divert our attention to a new and dangerous element that had arisen behind our lines. We were losing men from hidden snipers who were shooting our troops in the back. They had killed our men in several areas, including Kapasan, Tunjungan and Embong Malang, where the clandestine Rebel Radio studio was located. We knew some parts of Surabayan society who from early times were favored under the Dutch colonial rule and felt it would be to their advantage to help the British bring the Dutch back.

To counter the snipers, we asked all kampung people to carefully watch our rear ground for outsiders moving among them. They succeeded in catching several snipers in their midst by doing intensive searches. Before long several of these sharpshooters were flushed out and dealt with. They were pro-Dutch Chinese, quite different in their attitudes to the third and fourth generation Chinese who had made Surabaya their home.

DAPUR-2 UMUM: COMBAT KITCHENS

The logistics of food supplies worked well in the first week. The communal kitchens were in kampungs at our rear, where it was relatively calm, though sometimes threatened by artillery or aircraft machine gunfire. The women who kept the kitchens working, as well as supervising their gradual relocation south, were true heroines.

In the narrow laneways called *gang* other households helped the fighters by leaving on their doorsteps small packets of cooked food, wrapped in fresh banana leaves held together with bamboo needles, and small bottles of fresh water. British soldiers going along those paths were oblivious to these innocent-looking banana leaf parcels, but for us they were valuable acts of solidarity from the people. They were precious gifts that boosted morale, as did the mysterious but famous Imam of Blauran Lane. He was an elderly Kiai religious scholar who arrived unannounced and set up a little space in Blauran Lane No 1, where he gave prayers and a sip of "holy water" to the young fighters. Very soon this kindly man had attracted so many teenage fighters that they formed lines to visit and receive a kind word. His holy water was like liquid gold for the young fighters whose nerves were fraught after being subjected to several days of relentless onslaught and the spectre of death hanging over them.

Bung Tomo skillfully used the story of this religious scholar handing out blessed water as propaganda over Rebel Radio. In his fiery speeches he said he had imagined the Kiai was really a man of magic and used his magic powers to fly in from Malang to help out.

Just who he was and where he came from, no one discovered at the time, and it was many decades before his identity was known. His spiritual sustenance to the fighters ensured he was fondly remembered. The British began bombing Blauran Lane and he was finally forced to move. They had mistaken the long lines awaiting his blessing for a consolidation of forces.

WE MOVE A LITTLE SOUTH

On 14 November we moved the defensive lines back to Pasar Besar, our biggest marketplace, and Jagalan, Kawatan, Marpati and Pasar Turi. We held this line with five days of continuous fighting. On the western side of the Pasar Turi market, small squads of our fighters supported by our Military Police troops were holding out on the west bank of the Pegirikan Canal. In Asam Jajar we succeeded in punishing the British who retreated, leaving many fallen troops and weapons.

The shelling from warships was thunderous and constant, reaching as far south as Simpang Lonceng. Our intelligence reports told us the British had moved their ships westward of their original positions in Tanjung Perak, perhaps to be within reach of new targets. Their use in combat of regular-sized tanks diminished, perhaps because of the "dare to die" street fighter attacks that had demolished several of them and their crews.

On Thursday 15 November 1945 the fighting on day six raged in all sectors including Contong Square, Gemblongan district, the Great Marketplace, Semut and Kapasan. In pockets of slum kampungs behind enemy lines, our concealed street fighters with grenade launchers "harvested" more enemy lives.

While we didn't have a radio network to direct our troop movements, the defense units remained immobile. There was no central command system, instead we had a system of "latitude" guidance for commanders wherein each company was given latitude to develop initiatives, providing they included plans to "deceive, attack, confuse and kill" the enemy. Territorial divisions were never hard and fast because the kampungs each comprised a series of twisting and turning paths and lanes, and pockets of small public squares.

Entering week two of the Battle on Saturday 17 November 1945 the British fighters strafed a locomotive in Gedangan, killing many passengers. They also attacked Sidoarjo Station, 24 kilometers inland south of Surabaya. Later, Wonokromo had its turn on the same day. Accurate fire from the British planes resulted in many killed and wounded. The aircraft attacks were increasing in frequency, indicating they had flown in reinforcements from Singapore or Malaya.

On Friday 16 November we ordered a general evacuation of women and the elderly. They did not fully comply because many wanted to stay and help defend their city, especially girls who helped their mothers with food preparation or worked in Red Cross posts. Even many children stayed, ignoring our instructions, even after seven days of bombardment.

It should be understood that many of our "soldiers" were teenagers and children from kampung families. They had to face the tall, bearded Sikh soldiers of the Mansergh Division on many occasion. One boy of about 15 who took aim at a bearded Sikh who suddenly appeared before him got a shock when his gun would not fire. The Sikh, in a humane gesture, approached the scared boy and gently took the gun away, telling him with "Mama" sounds and hand signals, to go home to his mother.

Governor Surio said of our juvenile soldiers, "These children are convinced they are protected by God Almighty...they fight for justice and truth. Every road and every building they defend with all their might. And if they can no longer defend, they burn. They too would rather see Surabaya become a sea of fire than see it a prosperous city in enemy hands." The city burned unabated, from incendiary bombing and artillery or from our own scorched earth tactics in places. The big gas factory at Semut burned for three days.

Surio promised that we were fighting to end an era. The Battle of Surabaya could not be delayed or avoided. The Battle was a harbinger of a dazzling era that would embrace all Indonesia.

Bung Tomo channeled the people's anger. While cursing the British and the Dutch, he also raised the fighting spirits of patriots all over Indonesia with his fiery speeches, which were often just angry diatribes urging his listeners to "burn their houses, until they run helter-skelter." Bung Tomo, however, was a reluctant soldier who rarely set foot outside his studio, or took up arms to join the fight. He ended his speeches with several "Allahu Akbar" calls. Two years after the Battle for Surabaya he posed in uniform in a Malang resort hotel for a Jakarta magazine, striking a defiant posture as though leading troops. The image flooded the Internet, with photo-shopped fireballs added for November 10 posters. The truth was Bung Tomo was more valuable to us in his Rebel Radio studio than fighting on the streets.

On Sunday 18 November 1945 the fighting flared with even more intensity, and for us slightly more successfully because we had learned so much during the first week of fighting. The tanks and panzers were good, but limited in their capacities. Their machine gunners risked running out of ammunition, and shells for their cannon were quickly exhausted. Their small fuel tanks limited their range and the drivers' views were through a narrow window with almost no peripheral vision.

Because of that the tanks needed infantry to follow and protect them in the narrow streets and lanes of old Surabaya, where their maneuverability and speed was limited. During the first week or more of fighting these arenas of densely settled old kampungs were not only hazardous for panzers but soon became their burial ground. The *jibaku* dare-to-die squads used the weak points to attack the enemy crews when the panzers were in confined spaces, dropping hand grenades through the tank cockpit. These boys were often killed in the attempt, but many jumped clear after successful strikes. They dared to die, but escape was always preferable.

SURABAYA DEVASTATED: BUILDINGS IN RUINS. STREETS QUIET.

The resulting debris from the fighting could be seen over all fields of combat, where half-ruined or completely flattened buildings were evident. The famous areas of Pasar Turi, Kapasan, Semut, Pengampon, Jagalan, Peneleh, Pasar Kembang, Tamarindelaan, Pasar Besar and Kebalen were in shambles. A very large godown in the heart of the Pengampon kampung area was completely destroyed and hundreds of houses built along 13 narrow laneways burnt down, sending inhabitants scrambling and flaring their hatred of the British even higher.

In districts like these, there was frequent man-to-man, house-to-house and in-building fighting along narrow pathways and lanes, which was very tricky. The sounds of shots were continuous, but detecting their origin was difficult because of the echoes from ricocheting rounds bouncing from walls.

Our artillery units, despite not being organized into batteries, were able to niggle the enemy. Our cannon were mixed, from AA guns, field guns, and beach cannon all in the hands of former Heiho Japanese trained troops. Several of them learned their skills when serving as auxiliaries to the Japanese Army in Thailand, though most of the men sent overseas did not survive. Many of our boys volunteered to man these, though none of them had any experience using them. Enthusiasm was their only qualification.

HAMMERED ARTILLERY ACCUSE BUNG TOMO
OF A LOCATION LEAK

One artillery team criticized Bung Tomo for letting slip on radio the location of their artillery units in Wonokromo, claiming we were hitting enemy positions in Ujung and Tanjung Perak. When they said the British used Rebel Radio coordinates calculated by monitoring his broadcasts, he looked incredulous, and happily exclaimed, "You're not saying the British *believe* me?" (*Mosok Inggeris percoyo aku!*)

By Monday 19 November Governor Surio had determined our military and humanitarian situations to be dire, and advised Jakarta so. The Simpang general hospital was overflowing. Patients were being forced to flee to Sidoarjo, Kertosono, Kediri, Mojowarno, Malang and other places inland, to the safety of rural East Java. Doctors and paramedics had streamed in from outside Surabaya, but the numbers were insufficient. The British had succeeded in occupying the northern half of the city and were restricting our movements, forcing our withdrawal to the southern sector.This was the newer part of Surabaya, not as crammed with small streets and lanes. Streets further south were wider such as Tunjungan Road, Embong Malang, Keputran, Gemblengan, Praban, and Kedung Doro and there were fewer kampung complexes. This was the district on the west bank of the Kali Mas, where the British infantry could more easily coordinate their movements with tanks.

After taking ground in the Great Marketplace of Pasar Besar, the British chose to concentrate forces into a new line of attack, advancing to Wonokromo on the West Bank of the Kali Mas. Although it was proving more difficult, our forces were still attacking some enemy positions; the most lauded of our kampung fighters, because of their fanaticism, were in Kranggan, Tunjungan, Kapasan, Kapasari, Gemblongan, Sawahan and surrounding areas, all densely settled kampungs.

The Battle was in its eleventh day on Tuesday 20 November 1945 when there unfolded what was to be one of the final tempestuous firefights during which both sides took heavy losses. We suffered losses in the defence line districts of Embong Malang, Kedung Doro, Kedung Klinter and Pandegiling. The other areas of action were the districts of Kranggan, Praban, Genteng Kali, Plampitan, Tunjungan, Kaliasin, and Pregolan. These were not well-coordinated actions directed from our headquarters or command posts. We were unable to do that. Any synchronization of action by our men was coincidental, usually arising from their common desire to fight until the last, shouting, "Merdeka atau Mati! Freedom or Death!"

Our strength was in our young men, who with each day seemed to mature dramatically. Their faces saddened in the quieter evening hours as they saw their ranks thinning day by day and they feared they might be next. They had developed, despite or *in spite* of these fears, enough confidence to make decisions without awaiting orders. The physical composition of their squads and platoons varied in strength and skills, making them flexible, formidable foes in close proximity warfare. Their only commonality with their more experienced colleagues was their determination to be free. Their spirit flowed over into all aspects of civilian life, and when they came back to their own kampungs for a break their presence was like an electric charge. They gave even the oldest residents new hope and confidence in a future, a different life that for decades under the Dutch felt like one tough year after another, and got even worse under the Japanese.

How was it with the British? Were they comfortable with their role in defending a Dutch colonial rule and being compared unfavorably to the Japanese Army? Were the British deliberately using their Indian Division and Gurkhas because they knew that English, Scottish and Irish personnel wanted to return home after so long at war? After all, the Japanese had surrendered three months ago. Many Britons regarded the war in Indonesia as dishonorable, and within the infantry ranks there were differing shades of attitudes and opinions.

On the other hand, a number of the Indian troops deserted British ranks and came over to us. We promised them, rather rashly, an idyllic village life and marriage to a pretty young Javanese. Our propaganda was designed to make the Indian Moslem soldiers uneasy about their part in killing Indonesian Moslems. We had only marginal success. Very few Indians deserted and very few of those who did stayed on after 1945.

On Wednesday 21 November, the twelfth day of what was now known worldwide as the Battle for Surabaya, we made a last ditch effort to coordinate the administration of our forces and incorporate the large number of new volunteers as they arrived from other parts of Java. The new body was the Council of East Java Indonesian People's Struggle, which we abbreviated to the "DPRI". The DPRI announced said they would guide and inform the people by using traditional bargaining and consultation methods called *musyawarah* and *kegotongroyongan*. The thrust behind the umbrella body was to tackle the lawlessness that had arisen in these desperate last days of the Battle, where armed hotheads were inclined to seek violent solutions for their problems. The new decrees were:

1. The people of Surabaya may not take law into their own hands and pass sentence on those suspected of wrongdoing.
2. All matters connected with sentencing must be directed to the DPRI.
3. All those now held in detention by the people must quickly be handed over to the DPRI East Java.
4. Those disobeying these instructions will be severely punished.

Innocent people had been falsely accused and "sentenced" by the masses. The accusers had too often succeeded in escaping justice.

SHERMAN TANKS ENTER THE EQUATION

The same day, the British brought in Sherman tanks, which altered the equation, putting them into the field on 23 November, which seemed a bit late. The Shermans were used to destroy bunkers and sandbag defenses, repeatedly reversing over them, and then withdrawing while the offshore shelling and aerial bombing pounded suspected *Arek* strongholds. These massive, powerful machines were trouble for any enemy force, let alone one poorly equipped and lacking experience in modern warfare. The Shermans dominated the boulevards and caused us to change our tactics. They took no time at all to close in on us in southern Surabaya, by using our north-south roadways.

Some troops from the front line areas had stayed behind in Tunjungan, Kranggan, Pregolan and Embong Malang, intending to slow the advance down, but the Shermans comfortably took care of them.

The older part of town had by now become relatively calm, with only sporadic gunfire sounding. Very few people were seen moving around. Outside the closed doors of many kampung houses the parcels of food left out for our fighters remained uncollected. The communal kitchens were withdrawing to the south, following the main forces as they went into a strategic retreat.

THE OLD TOWN QUIET. OUR FORCES RETREAT SOUTH

By Saturday 24 December, Day 15 of the Battle, our front line was pushed back to the Embong Malang district. Sarkies Hotel, the former Dutch NIROM radio building and some others our last main bases of defense. We took down the rear, south-facing fences of properties we were using to make unimpeded, quick retreats. Enemy aircraft returned to bombing again and the tank fire directed at us was intense, though indiscriminate. I heard talk about, but did not witness, several young fighters preparing suicide attacks on tanks. Most of the earlier "dare-to-die" fighters had used grenades or explosives in attacks that had been made in the hope of hurting tank crews but surviving to fight another day. I was never impressed by this form of warfare and did not advocate such methods within my ranks.

In this last phase the British used the road along the west riverbank to press forward, starting at Kayoon, then through to Keputran, Dinoyo, and Darmo Kali and up to the Wonokromo Bridge. Using these tactics, the British avoided kampung-based reprisal attacks. This exerted tremendous pressure on us, forcing us to retreat. We suffered very heavy losses, both dead and wounded. The courageous women on what we euphemistically called the "Night Duties" were dismayed and discouraged by the numbers of dead and broken bodies left behind requiring quick wrapping and burial.

We had to keep moving south, but the Kali Mas waters upstream were both wide and deep, a formidable natural obstacle to cross if we were to try fighting back using the vast kampung complex on the east riverbank as protection. The problems were mounting and we had to face the reality of withdrawal while minimizing our losses that were now all too evident to us.

HARDSHIPS IN RETREAT:
FOOD AND MEDICINES IN SHORT SUPPLY

We persisted with the communal kitchens, though by now the quantity and standard of food was low. Bung Tomo via Rebel Radio appealed to regional people to send food to Surabaya. The response was extraordinary. Trains heading for Surabaya were packed with foodstuffs and we lost a lot to spoilage because we couldn't spare the manpower to collect them. We had control of the Central Java to Surabaya line, so the station masters along the way carried food donations gratis.

The last safe station for unloading food was Wonokromo. When everything was functioning, Ibu Prangko who was in charge directed the trucks by hand signals to drivers transporting prepared food to the combat zone.

MEDICAL EMERGENCIES

By the second week of fighting, care of the wounded had become a major problem. The hospital authorities requested we search for medical supplies the Japanese were rumored to have stockpiled, but we found none. It was a pressing problem, though alleviated somewhat by supplies from rural town hospitals in Sidoarjo, Mojokerto and Malang. Sidoarjo was just an hour south, but Mojokerto was half a day and Malang, deep into East Java, a full day's travel by rail or the damaged and clogged roads.

No matter how many of our street fighters fell, it had little effect on the continuous flow of volunteer fighters from outside Surabaya. An estimated 20,000 to 30,000 volunteers from all over Java had come into Wonokromo station, or by road to Jombang, Gresik, by boat from Madura, or Pasuruan via ferry from Bali. At its peak, mid-battle, hundreds were arriving by the hour, including young women answering the radio calls to help in hospitals. No experience was needed, just a desire to fight for independence. Volunteer nurses immediately went into exhausting shifts at hospitals in an attempt to cope with the wounded.

The roads outside resembled an abattoir. Blood drenched the roadways; victims screamed out in pain, many of them were limbless. Since the end of October the dead were so numerous they had been taken away for speedy burials, according to Muslim custom, whether identified or not. No one knew how many disappeared in this way. In one particularly damaging strike, we lost 300 people.

The wounded were taken to the Central Hospital where day by day the numbers had mounted. The Karangmenjangan Hospital, formerly the Japanese Naval Hospital, now under Doctors Sugiri and Rustamaji, was soon unable to cope. Several other city hospitals, including the William Booth, Catholic, Japanese

Civilian Hospital and a second Japanese Naval Hospital in Undaan, faced the same inundation of the wounded.

The morale of the nursing staff working virtually non-stop, night and day, was difficult to maintain. Although their spirits were high their physical energies were drained and they often simply dropped to the floor and fell into a deep sleep. Journalist Rosihan Anwar, our first War Correspondent, wrote later that he saw exhausted staff sleeping on floors and along corridors. Anwar was reporting for *Merdeka* newspaper and had travelled by train into Wonokromo station from Yogyakarta on a train bringing ammunition. He was the first to report to the outside world that we had control of most of rural East Java and that the Indonesian flag was flying in every village station he passed. Hundreds of villagers had swarmed onto the train stations along the way, shouting, "Merdeka! Merdeka!" and raising their fists to salute him, as he watched from inside his train carriage. Jakarta had known nothing of this. The politicians, headed by President Sukarno, were holding a Youth Conference in Yogya. They learned of the fighting in Surabaya after a phone call from T. D. Kundan.

To overcome the acute staffing problem, a senior hospital administrator, Dr Soetopo, called for volunteers on RRI Radio Republic Indonesia and Rebel Radio. So many young women came to give their time that soon we had more volunteers than the hospitals could manage. Among the new arrivals were nurses who had travelled three days from as far as West Java and South Sumatra, many of them trained in First Aid during the Japanese years. They were affectionately known as "Pi-pi-kahs," our friendly term for the PPPK whose organization was the *Pertolongan Pertama Pada Kecelakaan: First Aid in Accidents,* and all were unpaid volunteers. They were the foundation staff for our biggest public hospitals and because of their intensive Surabayan experience were often rapidly promoted to senior posts when still in their twenties. The number of rooms for emergency surgery was increased but there were never enough to cope.

The Battle for Surabaya had been our life for what seemed years, but had been just two weeks. We had been in civilian or military combat mode for one hundred days if we counted from the Day of Flags on 22 August and included the Tambaksari meeting, the weapons raids on Japanese compounds, the street fights against returning Dutch internees, the storming of the Kempeitai in October, the first bloody fighting to remove the British occupation in late October and the days of preparation between the ceasefire rejecting the British Ultimatum.

THE BRITISH REACH THEIR SOUTHERN LIMITS

In the final days of fighting within Surabaya's city limits, we fiercely opposed the enemy advance with all our strength, but the Sherman tanks and panzers dominated the conflict. They took the important strategic sectors north of Pandegiling Road, east of Dinoyo Road, west of Kembang Kuning Road and south of the Zoo in Wonokitri and Ketintang.

The British mobilized their Shermans and fighter-bombers to attack us relentlessly over two more days until Tuesday 27 November but we made it as tough as possible for them to take territory from us. We withdrew under pressure south and east, fighting desperately to the southernmost limits of the city.

On Wednesday 28 November 1945 our Eastern Sector Defense also had to face reality and adjust to the new developments. Forces in such numbers could generally only move south, but at the time the area south was wet rice fields and broad fishponds and they chose not to cross those open areas because they would have been vulnerable targets. Small groups decided to retreat north via the kampungs of Pacar Keling, Kapas Krampung and Rangkah, then head for Sidotopo and attempt to infiltrate into Surabaya after the British had departed.

SURABAYANS RETREAT THURSDAY 28 NOVEMBER 1945

The area around the zoo, Gunungsari and Ketintang was our last line of defence. Between Friday 30 November and Sunday 2 December 1945, mainly student soldiers held this last line of defence at great cost. The enemy tanks destroyed much of the zoo and the Gunung Sari foothills. Ruslan Abdulgani later reported the Sumatran tigers were so frightened by the explosions they refused to leave their cages, even when their doors had been opened. Facing those sorts of pressures our fighters were forced to retreat, some towards Kedurus, Karang Pilang and Sepanjang and others toward Wonocolo and Waru. All the PRI youth units went via Rolak Songo (Nine Water Gates) then to Ketintang where the PRI youth headquarters was located and where they made a last ditch stand.

THE WAR ENDS

A soundless halt of enemy fire we intuitively interpreted as the end of the war. We...could stand upright, and walk freely...without being shot or bombed.

On Monday 2 December 1945 a strange silence fell over the battlefield, a soundless halt of enemy fire we intuitively interpreted as the end of the war. We somehow knew we could emerge from protective covering, stand upright, walk freely, cross a road and speak freely without being shot or bombed. We propped our weapons close to us and waited.

The Battle for Surabaya had been our life for what seemed like years, but had been just three weeks. We had been in civil revolt or military action for three full months if we counted the attacks on the Japanese in September, the taking of the Kempeitai compound in October, and the three-day bloody clash with the British after they had occupied the city at the end of October.

We stared at each other, revealing mixed emotions of relief and happiness and sadness until sheer exhaustion overtook and immobilized us. The deeply seated residual tiredness that had lain in wait for us now rose to impact on all our senses and would stay with us until we could fully recover in the peaceful rural surroundings of East Java. We would soon take special moments to deal with the sorrow for those we had lost, for the territory we had temporarily given up, and for our own wounds and bruises, but that could wait. Many of us, especially the very young, were wandering around as sleepwalkers, somnambulant as we carried out a roll call or sought news of a certain friend's fate, or hoping that other friends in our unit had made it through alive, and remembering hundreds who had not.

EPILOGUE

After tempestuous fighting that had begun on 10 November as a punitive action, which the British generals in Jakarta said would last no more than three or four days, they had succeeded in driving us south of the Surabaya city boundary. Despite that win, the British were still not able to convincingly say they fully controlled the city of Surabaya. We still had small units operating inside the town who could niggle them. After the bitter experience of the Battle, the British would not be comfortable with the people of Surabaya, who were relentlessly desperate for their freedom and would surely turn to guerilla warfare.

The British were still doubtful of deploying any troops further south to chase down our troops because that would stretch their forces over an already broadening combat zone, and their supply lines would be vulnerable to guerilla attacks. The British could not hope for another Division of reinforcements because, thanks to the Battle for Surabaya, their troops were now facing a series of uprisings of pro-independence fighters in Central and West Java and Sumatra that were tying down their troops. Perhaps more importantly, they had done the job required of them. It was high was time they packed up.

The British soon made it clear they were in a hurry to leave and handed the city over to the Dutch NICA administration in March 1946. NICA brought the first Dutch troops into East Java on 9 March, but by then Surabaya was a shell of its old colorful, historic self, having lost around 80 per cent of its population. The formerly palatial residential homes and company headquarters, the most architecturally advanced in Asia, and exquisite shops on wrought iron laced avenues were now in tatters.

There would be more fighting, but the Republic was a fact now. From the Day of Flags on 22 August last, until now, we had been a free people in a free city. We had never expected the Dutch to leave without a fight and we were now preparing for a continued, longer fight, this time against a more fully equipped Dutch Army that would soon be back on Java. I saw the British assaults in Indonesia as *delaying action* to give time for the Dutch to rebuild their colonial army that the Japanese had destroyed in 1941.

After the Battle for Surabaya had ended, the Dutch quickly gathered the remaining troops of their Royal Dutch Army (KNIL) from internment camps in Java and Sumatra. Many of their former troops who had been shipped out of Java by the Japanese to Burma, Japan, Malaya and Thailand were gathering into new formations. Their recruiting and regrouping of troops was done in Malaya and Balikpapan in Kalimantan. Eurasians and former Dutch plantation workers were given priority entry in the army.

The stream of refugees from Surabaya into rural East Java was still evident at the end of the year, though now down to a trickle, the last of more than 400,000 who had left the city. We knew from our own experiences that tens of thousands of Surabayans had been killed and more than a 100,000 wounded.

When the Japanese had arrived at Wonokromo Bridge in March 1942, Surabaya's official population was 618,000. Where we stood now, near the railway and main road out of the city, 409,000 refugees had passed through, heading south to get to inland towns in Republican hands. Those who fled the city after their homes and possessions were obliterated would rarely return to Surabaya, preferring to start a new life in a lovely town like Malang, or perhaps a quiet village. Surabayan evacuees soon comprised 50 percent of the population in several hinterland towns.

After a rest we would prepare for the defense of the hinterland, going to the mountains if necessary. I took a squad into the Kawi Mountains and from that base conducted several successful ambushes on convoys. We had anticipated a continuation of the struggle and as far back as October had transferred ammunition and explosives from warehouses in the city as well as the ammunition the Japanese had stored in Batuporon on Madura Island to Mojokerto, Kediri, Madiun, Malang and other strategic towns in East Java. We also took machine tools, lathes, electrical components, dynamos, laboratory equipment and useful chemicals such as arsenic, ammonia, nitric acid and potash alum for medicines and dyeing. We carried pharmaceuticals, medicines, surgical and hospital equipment, where we thought we could spare it. The evacuation was planned long before our forces were compelled to retreat from Surabaya and was a fine example of brilliant, strategic thinking. The lathes would be vital machines for us over the next years of struggle, to make light weapons, mines and grenade launchers, weapon repair, spare parts for vehicles and other useful items.

Another important facet of the evacuation was to successfully transport the wounded from the Simpang and other hospitals. This carried moral and psychological weight with the armed fighters as well as the common people, for troops fight better when they know they will be cared for if wounded. At the request of Dr Sutopo, doctors and paramedics were brought in from Jakarta and other towns, through the Indonesian Red Cross. Dr Suwandi handled the supervision of medical assistance. Dr Azis Saleh came from Jakarta with a team of medical students. Dr Garjito arrived with a volunteer team from Madiun. During the fighting the movement of patients was done mostly by night because daylight evacuation convoys were subjected to savage aerial bombing, but now we used any transport available, trains, trucks, private cars, becaks, horse drawn and ox drawn carts and human volunteers carrying the injured on their back. The trucks were from "BOM" (Barison Oeroesan Mobil) that later became the national public bus enterprise DAMRI.

Life after withdrawing south was not ideal. Sabarudin, the mean-tempered, jealous soldier who had tried my patience and tracked down and killed a talented, innocent man who had been photographed while a Boy Scout at a Jamboree hosted by Queen

Wilhelmina, didn't stop with the killing. He falsely accused anyone who crossed him, killing prisoners who were yet to go on trial. He became infamous for his cruel methods, often burning victims alive after dousing them with petrol, or dragging them behind a truck until their skin was stripped off, dying an agonizing death. After the East Java Military Police moved their headquarters to Sidoarjo, Hasanuddin confronted Sabarudin. Hasanuddin was Commander of the East Java Military Police Surabaya, now based in Sidoarjo, and Sabarudin had somehow been made Commander of the Military Police at Regency level, also headquartered in Sidoarjo. I was recovering from an operation to have shrapnel removed from my skull, so I missed the deadly confrontation. Sabarudin finally paid with his life for his pathological hatred and mania for torture.

I was in Yogyakarta in early 1946 when the State Secret Service (Badan Rahasia Negara Indonesia, BRANI) was being formed and heard they were seeking skilled staff. The acronym BRANI was a clever play on *berani,* which means 'courage', or 'fearless'. On the strength of my record in Surabaya, I was nominated, and gladly accepted the position. That was the start of a long career as a professional military officer.

But that is a story for another time.

AUTHOR'S NOTE

My close friend Hasanuddin was killed in the Second Dutch Military Action that they called 'Police Actions', to give the world the impression they controlled Java.

AFTERWORD

On 27 October 2000, the British Ambassador to Indonesia, Richard Grozney, expressed "regret" to the Indonesian people at a conference held by The Human Rights Committee for the Support of Victims of the 10 November 1945 Bombing.